GW00568809

Enfield Libraries

91200000382128

Photograph by Harry Stearns, San Francisco

SHOWMANSHIP
for MAGICIANS

By Dariel Fitzkee

Author of . . .

MISDIRECTION FOR MAGICIANS

THE ONLY 6 WAYS TO RESTORE A ROPE

THE STRANGE INVENTIONS OF DR. ERVIN

CONTACT MIND READING

CHINESE RING MANIPULATION

CUT AND RESTORED ROPE MANIPULATION

JUMBO CARD MANIPULUATION

Editor of . . .

BUCKLEY'S CARD PROBLEMS

Martino Fine Books
Eastford, CT
2017

Martino Fine Books
P.O. Box 913,
Eastford, CT 06242 USA

ISBN 978-1-68422-106-6

Copyright 2017
Martino Fine Books

All rights reserved. No new contribution to this publication may
be reproduced, stored in a retrieval system, or transmitted, in any form or
by any means, electronic, mechanical, photocopying, recording, or otherwise,
without the prior permission of the Publisher.

Cover Design Tiziana Matarazzo

Printed in the United States of America On 100% Acid-Free Paper

SHOWMANSHIP
for MAGICIANS

By DARIEL FITZKEE

Author of . . .

MISDIRECTION FOR MAGICIANS

THE ONLY 6 WAYS TO RESTORE A ROPE

THE STRANGE INVENTIONS OF DR. ERVIN

CONTACT MIND READING

CHINESE RING MANIPULATION

CUT AND RESTORED ROPE MANIPULATION

JUMBO CARD MANIPULUATION

Editor of . . .

BUCKLEY'S CARD PROBLEMS

Published by SAINT RAPHAEL HOUSE

San Rafael, California

COPYRIGHT 1943
By DARIEL FITZROY

Dedicated to my friend,
DR. DOUGLAS M. KELLEY,
who as Captain with the
United States Army overseas,
even now as this is being written,
is enriching a career I have
long watched with admiration.

TABLE *of* CONTENTS

─────────

i

CONTENTS

CONTENTS

CONTENTS

CONTENTS

CONTENTS

INTRODUCTION

The fact that I feel there is to be a definite need for this book is evidenced by my having written it.

While this work is intended primarily for magicians, there is very much here, particularly the analysis of audience preferences and appeals, which applies to entertainers generally.

There is a right way and a wrong way of doing anything. But the right way of yesterday is not necessarily the right way of today.

The following pages, of course, set forth only my viewpoint on magic presentation. It probably is not a particularly good viewpoint, I am reasonably certain, since I have been assured of this both directly and indirectly by many who know nothing whatever of the matter. On the other hand some people of intelligence and experience in the theatre world seem to feel as I do, which is one of the reasons I have dared to undertake this book.

The classic retort: "Well, he's working," is not necessarily conclusive nor unanswerable in connection with comment on an entertainer's offering. It might be answered that a burglar is working, and for profit, while he is in the act of drilling someone's safe.—And while honest men starve. The phrase is not justified economically or morally.

The mere fact that a man is working may be due to many factors. He may have friends of influence. His compensation may be comparatively low. Someone else might be making a special profit by keeping him working. His publicity, not his abilities as an entertainer, may be keeping him employed.

That a man is employed now does not mean he will continue to be engaged if he fails to keep abreast of the times.

The arrangement of words herein and a great many of the ideas developed are mine. The facts, which are a contribution

1

from the show business as a whole, are the property of no one person. They belong to the Theatre which discovered them bit-by-bit.

There is one type of audience appeal I have not included in my lists. These days it has been found profitable. I refer to the off-color and ribald. Where it is permitted, it is a powerful appeal. I must insist I am not a moralist. But I feel that off-color material is definitely damaging to the show business. Sooner or latter it will cause serious trouble. I refuse to include this appeal because it is a false one, spawned from the underworld, and eventually it will be driven back.

I firmly believe the good showman will detour around it carefully, holding his nose. I strongly advise it.

Finally, this book is the first in a trilogy which I eventually hope to complete. Like this one, the others are intended to cover unexplored territory. Much of the research on the two remaining volumes, both in entirely different spheres from this one, has been completed. Whether they shall ever be put in form for ultimate publication will rest very much on the sort of reception received by SHOWMANSHIP FOR MAGICIANS.

DARIEL FITZKEE

San Rafael, Calif.
October 19, 1943.

SHOWMANSHIP *for* MAGICIANS

CHAPTER ONE

It seems inevitable that sooner or later someone must take up the matter of showmanship and presentation for magicians in a detailed manner. Too many performers of magic, increasingly so in recent years, either do not know or totally disregard the fundamentals of modern entertainment as exemplified elsewhere throughout the amusement industry.

Years ago Dr. Wilson said. "Magic is an art that sometimes instructs, often amuses and always entertains." This writer disagrees emphatically with very much of that statement. Particularly does he question the "often amuses and always entertains" part. He is inclined to think that the doctor was somewhat carried away with his enthusiasm for a hobby.

It is a pretty set of words. But an ugly infection.

In my belief he would have been more nearly correct had he written, "Magic, as exhibited by the majority, is the indulgence in a hobby which rarely instructs, seldom amuses and almost never entertains." Pure magic, as the presentation of a puzzle to be solved, particularly as performed by the too enthusiastic and poorly prepared devotee, almost never entertains anybody except the enthralled practitioner himself. And if this devotee is not watched, he is extremely likely to become an insufferable bore.

Unquestionably this attitude will meet with considerable disagreement. But the bulk of opposition will come from those with little experience.

The performance of magic is a minor branch of the entertainment field. We are not now here concerned with the collecting of apparatus or books, the manufacture of magical apparatus, the recreational hobby aspects or any other auxiliary activity connected with the general term magic.

Here we are entirely occupied with magic in its ultimate form. That form, of course, is its performance in the presence of spectators. In any other form it becomes research, exercise, recreation, hobby, or even a particularly exotic type of narcism.

Even if one of the alternative basic forms is the cause of a beginning in magic, sooner or later the doer-of-sleights or the collector-of-apparatus ventures outside his secret hideout and elects to "perform" for somebody.

Then it is that the damage starts.

Usually this type of "magician" is inadequately prepared and quite without any right to consider himself an entertainer in any degree. Of the thousands of performers-of-tricks who daily exhibit their wares throughout the world, but a minute percentage has given any thought to presentation or showmanship which is the heart-beat and the life-blood of the entertainment field.

Yet just because this tyro's exhibitions may be limited to but a few admiring and, let's hope, forgiving friends or relatives, the writer must insist that he still has no right to do so without some intelligent preparation in selling entertainment to an audience, **whether his audience is large or small.**

The chief trouble is that the damage is not personal only. It is not limited to the bungler himself. It goes much further than that. It hurts all magicians as entertainers. And it injures all magic as entertainment.

Take the number of exhibitions of magic that are given throughout the country in a single day. This means all of them— good, mediocre and poor. Fully seventy-five percent of the performances are poor according to modern entertainment standards. Another twenty-four percent are mediocre.

The writer feels certain he is being conservative when he estimates that not more than one percent of the daily and nightly performances can be called smart and modern.

When ninety-nine percent of a product is poor or mediocre ALL of it is classed that way. That's why every poorly prepared magical performer hurts the entire field.

There is much tolerance for magicians as a group. Spectators are generally inclined to overlook the short-comings of the magician probably because of some psychological conditioning germinated during childhood. Yet this very favorable circumstance reacts as a considerable disadvantage. It creates too easy opportunity for the incompetent to inflict himself upon an utterly unwarned audience.

Of course, all people in an audience are not favorably inclined towards magic. Many people have experienced extreme boredom as the result of poor presentation in the past. Others regard the challenge to their wits, and the fact that they are frequently ultimately deceived, as a reflection upon their own acuteness. This carries with it the implication that the person accomplishing the deception is of superior mentality. This type of spectator distinctly resents such a situation.

Still another type of spectator simply is not interested. He is not interested in puzzles or trying to solve them. He is not interested in the mental effort. To him, such endeavor is just the opposite of relaxation. And this type of person is in the majority by far.

This is provable conclusively by the magazine field, which is printed entertainment. Are the magazines filled with puzzles? Or **narratives?** Are they most interested in things? Or **people?**

Spectator attitudes towards the presentation of tricks are complex and varied. In speaking of the presentation of tricks I am now referring to the generally accepted method of presenting magic. What is meant by this is the exhibition of magical effects solely as mysteries as to method of accomplishment, as paradoxes, as accomplished impossibilities or as puzzles.

The child, the adult with juvenile mentality, and the hobbiest look upon the challenge eagerly. Certain mental types who gain their relaxation through a change in mental activity look upon the solution of puzzles, whether in the form of tricks or mystery stories, as a form of mental refreshment. People who have a strong sympathy with childhood and the things of childhood respond to magic.

But the friends of magic itself, the magic of the performance of a simple mystery, as a puzzle alone, include but few in addition to the list above.

A man who was once called the greatest agent in the show business remarked to me that the customers for a magic show now were only "kids, bohunks and magic nuts." At one time he was the agent for what was then the greatest magic show in existence. I believe this man's judgment is sound.

But it is obvious that magicians have only themselves to blame. The Thurston show was at one time known as the most valuable property in the show business. No magic show even remotely approaches that status now.

Obviously, magic itself is not to blame. It attained this distinction once. It attained this distinction **when its method of presentation was geared and attuned to the times.**

That particular method of presentation, so successful once, is no longer suitable. It is not in key or in sympathy or in tempo with what is now the modern concept of entertainment, or with what the present-day public seeks.

"If your principal can so present a magic show that it once more appeals to the masses, he will be greater than Thurston, or Herrmann, or Houdini." This remark was made by another nationally prominent theatre executive to one of our agents during my experience with the International Magicians In Action show. He added, "And he'll make a fortune."

Subsequently, both agents expressed the belief that we had achieved the desired formula in that show.

Parenthetically, it might be stated that those who are familiar with the actual history of the show know its difficulties were not caused by the character, the slant or the material in the production, or its artistic side. Rather its progress was impeded by entirely insurmountable commercial obstacles and lack of sufficient capital to allow it to be opened in the only environment which would supply it with the necessary prestige and publicity opportunity. Sufficient funds were not at hand to take it to Broadway in order to properly build and exploit it as we knew it should be done. That show never had its chance.

However, through this experience and in view of the reactions available through its receptions by audiences and from many theatre executives, it does supply the foundation for many of the examples to be cited later in this text. If references to this show appear frequently, it will be understood I hope that it furnished the writer an opportunity to put his knowledge, limited, it is admitted, and theories, unlimited, perhaps it may be regretted by the reader, to practical application in an endeavor to gear magic to modern entertainment standards.

6

Marco, of Fanchon and Marco, said when he saw the show, "In its present form it is a good show—definitely a good one." Remember, he was speaking as an experienced theatre man, rather prejudiced against magic than interested in it, as so many professional theatre men are. "It can be made a great show, I think, by the addition of a voice, perhaps the right type of girl numbers in keeping with the idea already there, and a few minor changes here and there."

Leo Morrison, one of the best agents in Hollywood, said, "If you could open this show on Broadway tonight, with the proper exploitation, it could become a national sensation in a few weeks."

Macklin Megley, director of many original Broadway successes had much the same opinion, as had Rodney Pantages and others of equal prominence in the motion picture and theatre fields.

These opinions are cited to show that apparently we were well on the way towards a solution of this problem of modernizing magical presentation, although we may not have succeeded in evolving its final form.

But the individual performer need not become alarmed that this text is to be devoted to methods of making a full evening, big theatre magic show palatable to the seeker for entertainment. That is not the intention. However, the principles are the same, whether the entertainment is a six-minute night club turn, a two-hour program by a single performer, the performance of an elaborate legitimate theatre production, or the presentation of a pocket trick for an acquaintance.

This book seeks to discover what is objectionable, according to modern standards, in the usual presentation of magic at present. It seeks to discover why magic is no longer popular with the masses. It seeks to take apart other types of successful entertainment to find out what makes them popular.

It seeks, then, to apply these principles to magic performance.

But it also endeavors to impart to magicians generally the fundamentals of showmanship in such a manner that magic presentation may be improved from the spectators' viewpoint, whether in the performance of a single simple pocket trick for a solitary friend, an act for a club or a night club, or a full evening's show, alone or with a large company.

That it can accomplish this entire purpose is almost an impossibility, the writer freely admits. But it may clear the way in such a manner that subsequent writers on this subject may find the route a bit less difficult.

This can be the most important reading a magician ever did, even if the only thing the reader gets from it is an urge to look upon his magic performance objectively, as his spectators see it.

CHAPTER TWO

Let's look at this activity we call magic performance. Let's try to see it as it appears to the public. I'm afraid it isn't a pretty sight according to modern standards.

It must be borne in mind throughout this text that the writer is compelled to select the **usual** or average example in these discussions. There are smart performers. There are some, comparatively few it must be admitted with regret, who have adapted their offerings to modern standards. With these, of course, the writer has no quarrel. So where an occasional magician seems not to conform to the conventional picture that does not still alter the general over-all aspect.

This average magician that forms the subject matter of these discussions is a cross section of all who present magic. He is made up from the infrequent performer, the one who does just a few tricks to add variety to a social evening, semi-professional magicians, professionals and all others who elect to give exhibitions of their prowess. Because he is so many, made up from the ranks of the beginners, dilettantes, hobbiests, unskilled professionals and semi-professionals, and because, in contrast with these thousands, the really capable performers are so few, this cross-section by sheer weight of numbers establishes the standard. It is a standard which definitely reacts disadvantageously to the few who deserve better but who are automatically damned by the far more numerous general group.

To get back to the average magical performance:

One of the most unsightly and most dated pieces of furniture used by the average magician is his table. "Modern Magic" was published some seventy years ago. "The Modern Conjuror" was published in 1903. I have in my collection catalogues of Martinka & Co., Mysto and A. Roterberg, all published from 1910 to 1913. These center pedestal tables appear in all of these publications.

Particularly in the dealers' catalogues appear the typical magicians' tables of today, the tripod or Keller base, the center standard, black art tops, flat fringed drapes. Count the years back. It's a good portion of a century. Automobiles were made in 1910. How would one of those cars appear in modern traffic? How would your own personal attire date you if you were to don the garb of the gay nineties or the first decade of the twentieth century? What would a home look like if it were decked out in the bric-a-brac and furnishings of that overstuffed era?

Corn? If done seriously, yes.

You would instantly become a character if you habitually drove a 1910 automobile. If you wore clothes fashionable in the early part of the century. If your home were decorated and fitted out in that mode.

Characters of that type, thoughts of that era, decoration of that day become excruciating comedy today.

Then, why aren't the magic tables of that era out of date?

They are. But because magicians have been content to accept that era as the standard their tables date them and their craft in a damaging manner that labels magic itself as corn. Don't blame the dealers and manufacturers. They don't handle the goods you won't buy, if they're successful. The first fundamental of modern business is to handle the kind of wares the customers buy. Demand creates the supply in all cases. If magicians generally insisted on modern, smart tables the dealers would see that they were available.

But let's look at other tables that are in use today in the smart places. All of them are modern in design or adapted from certain classic designs, none of which even remotely resemble the atrocities we call magic tables. There are no gas-pipe center standards. What few center pedestal tables one sees are beautifully turned and finished designs based on genuinely beautiful and enduring patterns. Most of the tables are four-legged. The legs may be chrome-plated in keeping with certain types of moderne design. Or they may be wood in a variety of natural finishes. Incidentally, few pieces of furniture are painted and these are usually for breakfast nooks, gardens, kitchens and the more informal uses.

Notice also that none of them are painted gaudy red with violent contrasts in gold. That sort of a color scheme is circus art. Even the better circuses are getting away from that. Ringlings now employs Norman bel Geddes to design that show completely.

None of the furniture is draped with dark plush flat drapes. No modern drapery is decorated with gold stars or dragons. Occasionally, you see gold fringe. But not used as it is on magic tables.

Now let's look at the apparatus. Most of it looks like nothing else this side of heaven or hell. Huge black dice. Tin bottles painted black. Red and green and blue boxes gaudily daubed with wild and blatant designs in equally violent color contrasts. Nickle-plated cylinders. **Guns with funnels on the muzzle!** Funny looking stands and pedestals. Foulards that bulge, in designs that bring chills. Tie-and-dye silks and variegated scarfs went out twenty years ago. Flowers, among the most beautiful things on earth, positively do not look like those gaudily dyed feather dusters.

But this list is a long one. Page after page could be taken up in citing equally horrible examples. Look over your apparatus yourself. Examine it critically. Not as magical apparatus. But according to modern day standards. Just because it is magical apparatus is no reason it can violate the rules of present-day taste.

Why, this is stuff you work with. It is equipment that is plainly seen when you are supposed to be putting your best foot forward.

You violate the rules of fundamental good taste when you perform with apparatus that is flagrantly incongruous.

Again I insist, don't blame the dealers. Their business is to sell the kind of stuff you buy.

Perhaps much of this "dated" aspect is not entirely the fault of the magicians. Much of it could be psychological. Many of us received our first inspirations from "Modern Magic" and books of that vintage. Many of us received our first urges from watching professional magicians under the influence of that gay nineties era.

Thus, perhaps, were subtly formed standards which are now entirely out of harmony with these times. It must be admitted that much of this comes from childhood, and now that we are older we still stick to these standards in our second childhood.

That second childhood crack is not entirely wild, either. Many magical hobbiests spend considerable money for new toys under the guise of magic. Many hobbiests "play" by the hour with these

11

red wagons in a different form. This may account for the peculiarly childish tastes in apparatus, tables, silks and other accoutrements evidenced by so many magicians.

Now as to the dress: I have in mind at this particular moment a decidedly ludicrous picture. It is the photograph of a young man of perhaps twenty-eight. On his chin is a beard that resembles the adornment of an ambassador. It is black and luxuriant and curled in peculiar ways. This beard is entirely out of keeping with the character of the young man's face.

About this chap's head is wrapped a slightly soiled but obviously once white turban. The turban is adorned with a gilt star in front and some kind of a white plume. This young man is wearing a tuxedo of doubtful vintage. It looks a little tight in the legs. And it is certainly in a bad state of press. A long gold chain dangles in a loop from his trousers pocket.

The magician is standing in a painfully awkward attitude. His legs are spread apart with his somewhat bent knees quite prominent from the side view. He is resolutely, and not without some difficulty, trying to hold four billiard balls in his badly cramped left hand. The right hand clutches a wand with all of its remaining strength.

His thin hungry stomach is pushed out towards the nearby magicians' table. The table is conventional except that the drape is an American flag instead of the usual plush with stars and fringe. Upon the table is the obvious apparatus.

Now this chap has been trying to eke out an existence as a professional magician. He has succeeded in getting some bookings. Can you imagine the classification magic is getting from the spectators who witness his performance?

It matters little what skill he may possess. Long before he ever gets started on his routine, if he has a routine, his spectators peg him as a character. He conforms to every requirement of excruciating comedy, except one. The thing that prevents him from being terrifically funny to his audiences is his evident seriousness, his utter innocence of the fact that he is ludicrous. Generally audiences are collectively inherently kindly. The reason they do not rock with laughter is that there is a certain amount of pity developed.

12

But this type of character is not strange to magic.

Many magicians are characters to the spectators. Through peculiar hair-cuts, eccentric behavior, unconventional dress, lack of proper grooming, very bad conversation and talking habits, and multitudious crudities and peculiarities which so quickly illuminate an individual.

Many of them brag too much, lie too much, talk too loud. A great many of them are disagreeable in their attitude towards others. Many are absolutely without any care in personal grooming.

Fortunately, this type of character is in the minority. Yet it cannot be denied that these characters influence the average spectator's opinion as to magicians in general. Peculiarly, the disadvantageous characteristics such as these enumerated here weigh far more heavily in influencing the public than the circumspect behavior of the far greater majority. It is because they are so damnably conspicuous.

The type of dress the average magician wears during his performance is widely varied. The writer has seen performances in business suits, pressed and unpressed, in tuxedos that are smart and modern and in others that are woefully out of date. In dress suits that were new, pressed and up-to-date and in dress suits that were shiny with age and almost creaseless. In exotic costumes, national garb, in uniforms and in practically any state of dress. Some of these performers have had Paderewski haircuts, many of them were conventional. Some wore silk toppers and others turbans.

Probably the average performance in a business suit is done in a suit that needs pressing somewhat. Probably the average tuxedo or dress suit is somewhat out of date and ill-fitting. Probably the average performer is totally without make-up and most likely his hands are not even carefully groomed.

The usual term patter, used to denote the lines which go with the performance of a trick, is poorly chosen. The Funk & Wagnalls College Standard Dictionary defines "patter" as "Glib and rapid talk; idle chatter or gossip."

To this writer that does not characterize the verbal accompaniment that should go with modern magical presentation. The term, "lines," as used to connote the part spoken by an actor, seems far more apt.

The average "patter" at the average magical performance is usually more or less extemporaneous explanatory matter, elaborating unnecessarily on already obvious facts, delivered without any degree of skill. Or it may mean the rapid incongruities of some youngster, still speaking in a high-pitched squeak, babbling about his palpably non-existent trip to India or Egypt or some other equally impossible place for him.

Or it may mean the chattering of gags, whether or not they are particularly funny, or whether or not they apply to the immediate circumstances.—A delivery without any sense of the difficult arts of pointing and timing so essential to successful comedy.

It may mean the monotonous recital of some uninteresting fiction while all "lift" or "action" halts. Often it is delivered in a sort of a preoccupied monotone while the clearly bedeviled performer is concentrating his major attention on the doing of some finaglry connected with the operation of the trick.

Truly, the words uttered by the average magician during the average performance constitute the most dismal palaver ever inflicted upon an audience.

And then again, too often this colorless blabber is punctuated by an exhibition of stumbling and fumbling, while the performer worries about where to go, how to get there, how to stand, what to do with his hands, and whether the trick will work or not. In addition, this average performer never seems to know just where-in-hell his junk is.

There's too much stress on protecting the secret of the trick. Many performers deliberately get in front of their apparatus at a critical point in order to guard this precious secret.

No magic secret is worthy of being concealed if the effect cannot be done in normal manner out in the open so all may see. Magic is supposed to be **seen**.

No trick is worth performance if the secret of how it's done is more important than the impression it makes on the audience. That must be said again and again. It must be realized subconsciously every waking and sleeping moment of every day of every magician before magic can become genuine entertainment.

The secret hoarder is NOT a magician. He never will be a magician from the standpoint of being an interesting entertainer. These secrets aren't so damned valuable. There are few of them that can't be reasoned out by a man of fairly logical analytical ability.

It must be repeated again. The secret is NOT important. The ONLY thing that is important is its favorable impression upon the majority of the spectators.

Necessary to mention, too, are the assistants to the magicians. A very definite impression is made by the costumes, the grooming, the behavior, the characters and the actions of these aides. In this writer's experience the average assistant is inadequately trained, badly costumed, poorly groomed and not at all an asset.

Musical accompaniments are usually unsuitable, inexpertly scored, totally without cueing.

Thus, it may be seen that in this writer's opinion the average magical performer and his equipment is entirely out of step with modern entertainment standards. He could support this, if necessary, with more convincing proof from big time specialists in the entertainment field. I believe the majority of spectators would agree as well.

But you can satisfy yourself on this. Make it a point to attend performances of several first-class productions. Look at the product of the movies as represented in their more successful films. Look at the dress and behavior of these big time professionals, after they go through the meticulous criticisms of capable producers. Look at the devious ways, varied and unexpected, that favorable impressions are made. Listen to the music and watch how the performer responds. Study the delivery of lines and the pointing and timing. Study the material which has been selected for the performer to use. See how music and rhythm and many other appeals are brought into play to gain the favor of the audience.

Watch the reaction of the audience.

Now do you see what I mean when I criticize so severely the offerings of this average magician? Do you understand why I believe him to be an inadequate entertainer?

It was necessary to be somewhat severe in my analysis of the spectator's viewpoint of the average magician in order that a

15

logical approach may be made to overcome these deficiencies.

Consider your own choice of entertainment. **What do you honestly prefer?** Do you go to magic shows because they entertain you? Or because you are interested, as a magician?

I'll bet a slightly used mouth roll, like the rank and file, you too prefer lively songs, rhythmic dancing, hilarious comedy, tense drama, good looking girls, group coordination and all of the things featured by the more heavily patronized branches of the show business.

CHAPTER THREE

There are many ways of finding out what the public wants. Yet the simplest and most direct is undoubtedly through an investigation of what he buys. A man will accept almost anything for nothing, whether he likes it or not. But that isn't the condition when he has to part with his money for it.

Money, according to the value of his time, represents time spent in working. Whether a man spends his money or not depends upon his estimate as to whether what he is to get in return for his money is worth that much effort or not. The price he is willing to pay for anything, providing he is willing to pay something for it, establishes his value as to how much of his personal effort he is willing to sacrifice to obtain it.

Also, whether he is willing to buy and how much he is willing to spend, is a matter, to him, of his selection of the particular thing for which he wants to make this exchange.

The actual test must rest with a completely voluntary willingness on his part. There must be no coercion, strong, as in the case of a hold-up with a gun, or mild, as in the case of a solicitation for a charity, under pressure.

Then, becoming specific, the degree to which the public considers a show entertaining is reflected by the number of people that attend that show. This is, of course, also influenced by the admission charged.

It must be assumed in this reasoning that the show has not been misnamed in such a manner as to create a prejudice against it, or that the class of entertainment has not suffered in general because of past abuses.

Probably the greatest attendance, in numbers, is achieved by the motion pictures. This type of entertainment combines high entertainment value, low cost, exceptional selling campaigns and convenience.

Since we are not concerned here with the science of selling the public, and since we are not concerned with an analysis of making customer-acceptance convenient, we must discard these two latter ingredients in this work. It would be well, however, to keep them in mind, to be watched, so as not to be misled in our evaluation of customer preference.

We have said motion pictures combine high entertainment value and low cost. Of the two general types of pictures, dramatic and musical, undoubtedly the greatest attendance comes to the former. Therefore, at present we can assume that the general public prefers dramatic motion pictures first and musical motion pictures second.

Then would come stage musicals, with ice shows included in that classification, followed by stage dramatic shows. It must be borne in mind in connection with stage shows that they are much more expensive to the spectator. And for that reason those who are able to attend and those who are willing to buy must necessarily be less in numbers.

Next in general attendance, without bothering to obtain exact figures, would seem to be contests of all kinds—baseball, football, boxing, wrestling and so on.

Following this would probably be vaudeville and night club patrons with burlesque, opera, concert and ballet in that order.

It must be stressed that the writer has not investigated the exact order of attendance in these various classifications. These are broad, general estimates based on assumptions of the year's total business in each classification. A variation in their attendance order will have little bearing on what is to follow.

Let's look at this motion picture dramatic production field which the public finds so tremendously entertaining. It has a number of components which should interest us in our endeavor to discover what is entertaining.

Obviously. of course, there is considerable stress on known personalities. A dramatic story is necessarily a conflict between man and nature, or man and circumstances, or man and man, or man and himself. These classify into stories of achievement or of decision. The story is one of the struggle of a human being. This human being has certain character strengths and weaknesses. The character of the man and the type of obstacle he encounters determines the proponent's method of solving the difficulty. The spectator's interest increases with the importance of the outcome. To be superlatively dramatic the result must be of **vital importance** to someone.

18

As these problems approach problems which the spectator himself encounters in his everyday life they become more and more interesting to that spectator. It has been said by one of the prominent authorities that every popular story is about "a man in a hole and how he got out of it—or didn't."

Genuine drama results from an emotional conflict coupled with a character-revealing action on the part of one or more of the actors. An emotion is the outgrowth of a conflict between impulses within a person, resulting in a temporary deadlock. Character is revealed through three stages of action through which he goes when confronted by an obstacle. Everyone has some special way of immediate response, reflective delay and active response which identifies him as the character he is.

Therefore, people generally prefer for entertainment that which includes conflict, character and emotion.

Romance, which is an elemental conflict that always includes character and emotion, seems to be of greatest general preference. This is probably because it is common to almost all people.

But this film dramatic success almost invariably includes many general components. Of course, known personalities are used as the principle characters. There are conflict, character, emotion and romance, as stated before. Stress is placed on sex, common problems, sensations, complex situations and "escape" from the humdrum. There is almost invariably comedy. Many times nostalgia and sentiment are built up.

The productions show careful rehearsal and routine. The material has been tirelessly edited and selected. There is undoubtedly precision in the entire production.

And always at the end there is PUNCH.

The chief difference between the stage dramatic show and the film is that the film presentation generally puts stronger emphasis on sex appeal, with particular emphasis on romance. And, too, the film story has a carefully planned musical score.

Great care is revealed in the detail of the settings, the detail of the costumes, the make-up of the actors and in the careful personal grooming and dress of the actors, except for characters out of keeping with good grooming.

Film musicals are lighter in character than either types of drama. Almost without exception they carry a light plot, with

19

comedy foundation, and they stress music, singing, dancing, comedy, eye-appeal, romance, sentiment and sex appeal. All of the qualities present in the drama are present in the musical, but particular emphasis is placed on rhythm, youth, feminine beauty, sex appeal, music, melody, sentiment, nostalgia and novelty. Again, careful personal grooming, including make-up, is a particular feature.

Like the drama, the material is specially written, both lines and music. It is carefully edited, with the routines and scenes fast moving and short. When produced it is swiftly paced, expertly timed and painstakingly pointed. There are no waits or delays. There is no mumbling or fumbling. Neither are there any superfluous lines, movements or routines.

The show is unified throughout as to character, slant and all other qualities. Emphasis is placed on design, color, coordinated group movement and spectacle.

Football, baseball, boxing exhibitions and other contests feature one ingredient that is fundamental. That fundamental, also fundamental in drama, is conflict. But here the conflict is genuine. Added to this are known personalities, the stars. The further features are fast movement, sensations, action, crowds and drama-tense situations.

Vaudeville and night club entertainments feature youth, music, singing and dancing. There are heavy helpings of comedy, rhythm, sex-appeal. Music may be stimulating, nostalgic, sentimental, comic or romantic. The more successful individual acts invariably feature special material.

Usually the costuming is modern, smart and a bit extreme as to cut. No first-class performer would think of appearing without being faultlessly groomed and properly made-up. Everything must be clean and well-pressed.

The delivery is carefully timed and executed with precision and attention to pointing. Short turns, with fast pace, carefully edited and rehearsed, are the rule. Again there are no delays, fumbling, no excess lines or actions. Everything builds up, with purpose, to the final PUNCH. This final PUNCH is indispensible—whether for each number or for a final cumulative effect.

These acts actually are a fast succession of minor punches building to a supreme culminating WALLOP.

The chief features of burlesque are sex-appeal, low comedy, color, movement, music, rhythm, short scenes, fast action. Burlesque suffers because of less attention to detail, grooming, smartness and quality.

The opera offers names, music, spectacle and color. It includes crowds, movement, group coordination, careful rehearsal and routine. It suffers chiefly in public support in this country because scenes are too long, the movement is too slow and it is poorly paced and poorly edited.

The concert has little to offer the general popular audience except music and names.

The ballet has some of the features of the musical show, but comedy, sex-appeal, popular rhythm, romance, sentiment and other popular appeals are much less obvious.

Finally, the lecture field is confined to lesser known personalities with emphasis upon a single phase such as personality, accomplishment, experience or a unique feature.

Now in contrast, regardless of the field, let us examine a typical magic show.

No magician today equals the personal box-office appeal of a great many of the well-known stars of the theatre, screen and sporting field. This magic show features a single personality. There is very little sex appeal, except for the big magic shows and here it is poorly exploited. The music and rhythm and staging are poor. Chief reliance is placed upon mystery with comedy that has worn thin. The costuming, even in the biggest shows, is mediocre as compared with the leading attractions of the theatre or movies. The grooming and make-up are not up to professional theatre standards. Both the material and the comedy are conventional and often trite. The attack is slow, inadequately routined, with ineffective pointing.

Many magic shows suffer from poor material, poor delivery, fumbling, lack of precision, slow tempo, out-of-date ideas.

It doesn't seem to require a considerable amount of heavy analysis to discover why magic is not as popular as many other types of entertainment. The leaders in the more popular fields deliberately cater to the known preferences of the general public while the average performer in the magic field hasn't seemed to care and hasn't bothered to gear himself to popular demand.

21

Rather he seems to have insisted that the general public accept what he, the magician, wants to supply. Magic has retained the general style, the presentation, the type of material and the appearance it had, practically unchanged, at the beginning of the century.

But there is competition in this age. There is competition to obtain the consumer's dollar among the various classes of business. The clothing business tries to get it from the beverage business. The theatre interests try to divert it from the automotive channels. And so it goes.

Once that dollar reaches the entertainment field, there is further competition for it. The drama, the musical, the stage, the motion picture industry, other phases of the amusement field, all struggle for it.

After that the struggle is between types of acts or performers. Dancers, singers, strip dancers, impersonators, musicians, acrobats, magicians, dramatic actors—all enter the conflict to secure that money.

So, just as each industry tries to make that type of product attractive to the buyer, both as to product and price, so does each individual producer in that industry strive to make his particular product more attractive to the buyer than his competitor's.

It is the same among each type of entertainer. And from there it goes to the individual in each particular field.

There is plenty of justification for the magician to gear his entertainment to known customer preferences in entertainment. There is certainly ample reason why the magician must shape his product to approach that which the public prefers. That the magician, at this particular moment, is in a very low spot in entertainment preference in the general public opinion is inescapable. The demand for him and the compensation he gets, compared to demands for the services of other types of entertainers and their compensation, unanswerably proves the point.

We shall try to discover how magic may be shaped to modern entertainment standards. This cannot be done if only a few performers undertake the renaissance. The rank and file must make this change as well, each to the limit of his particular ability, before more favorable public demand will be evidenced. But it can't happen unless public preferences are catered to.

CHAPTER FOUR

You may take apart many successful productions, shows which have demonstrated that they were designed for the most public appeal, shows which have demonstrated this as proven by their box-office records, and you will find little in common with the usual magician's performance.

The choice may be made from any of the various branches of the entertainment industry—the stage, night-clubs, movies or the radio. Each stresses various aspects according to the limitations of that medium. During the old silent days the movies stressed facial expression, action and scenery. With the advent of sound the field was broadened to include all of the features of the living stage.

Obviously, "sight shows" are impossible over the radio at this time. It follows that the shows are limited to what may be imparted with sound alone. Space and perspective put some limitation upon what may be done on the stage. The character of the audiences, the business they are in and the limitations of the institution itself all influence the type of entertainment which may be seen at night-clubs.

But there are three types of entertainers which form the foundation of ALL of them. The movies, the stage show, the radio and the night-club all feature dancers, singers and comedians. And to some extent, in all of them except the night-club there is also drama.

Just what have dancers to offer in the way of appeal? Of course. rhythm and skill. Their performances show movement and physical action. Very often they feature youth. Most often they stress sex-appeal. Color and personality are evident. And very often comedy is paramount. In addition, the costumes are colorful, carefully designed and well-groomed. Make-up is invariably well done. And back-grounding it all is music.

Music, you must realize, carries with it psychologically grace, harmony, romance, sentiment, nostalgia—according to the type.

And the singers? All of the appeals possible through music as listed above—grace, rhythm, romance, harmony, sentiment, nostalgia. But in addition there is sex appeal again. And often comedy. Youth is frequently stressed. Likeable personality is important. The delivery of the song involves pointing and timing. Costume and make-up are particularly important.

Now the comedians: This is a very broad field, but generally there is some rhythm and music in every comedian's turn. Of great importance are pointing and timing and surprise. Often the crux of the comedy is dependent upon situation or character. Many of the comedians themselves play parts as characters. Personality is important. No first-class comedian overlooks the possibility of costume and make-up, in character with what he wants to seem to be to the audience.

Then drama: Drama, as has been said somewhat differently before in this work, is character and conflict. Personality is always vital. Often there is sex-appeal. And, too, the often-appearing qualities of romance, sentiment, nostalgia and comedy. Don't overlook the importance of make-up and proper costume.

From the above, then, we should be able to begin to cull a list of the often-found integrants in successful and popular entertainment.

Most often appearing in our analysis, as shown above, are the certain fundamentals:

1—Music	11—Sentiment
2—Rhythm	12—Nostalgia
3—Movement	13—Pointing
4—Youth	14—Timing
5—Sex-appeal	15—Surprise
6—Personality	16—Situation
7—Color	17—Character
8—Comedy	18—Conflict
9—Harmony	19—Proper costuming
10—Romance	20—Careful grooming

From the analysis of the various productions and methods of selling the material more fundamentals appear.

21—Physical action	30—Grace
22—Group coordination	31—Effortless skill
23—Precise attack	32—Sure-fire
24—Short scenes or turns	33—Spectacle
25—Efficient pacing	34—Thrill
26—Punch	35—Emotion
27—Careful routining	36—Common problems
28—Tireless rehearsal	37—Escape from the humdrum
29—Special material and score	38—Unity

Three types of faults common to amateur or poorly prepared entertainments are most carefully avoided. There are no delays nor fumblings. There are no excess movements or lines. Everything means something, everything builds-up to the climax without blind by-paths or diversions. The old rule of the show business is religiously observed: **Not too much; but just a bit too little.**

And there is that final, inescapable essential:

    39—Up-to-dateness

Now it may well be asked right here: How can all of those qualities be adapted to magic?

Before the writer attempts to answer that question it might be a good idea to go over that list with the AVERAGE magic entertainment in mind. Remember, now, I am not asking you to check this list with the qualities shown by a few of the top-flight professionals. The **average** magician is doing the harm, not the top-flight men. And I believe by this time you realize that the writer does not necessarily mean the man with the biggest magic show and the most apparatus is this top-flight man. The top-flight man will be found in the fastest company in the show business, the big revues, the best night spots, the movies. Here, he is competing with the best in the show business.

It must be realized that no one entertainer nor any single type of entertainment can possibly accomplish **all** of these popular appeals. Most obviously some of the basic ingredients are impossible. This depends entirely upon the type of act, the angle of approach, the type of audience the act or routine is intended for and the means available, through the circumstances of the personnel of the company or other influencing factors.

It is essential, however, that the individual performer attempt to gain as many of the important showmanship factors as possible. It must be done with discretion and a nice sense of values. Possibly material already in use can be so shaped and altered to fit many of the factors into the performance.

Try to get as many and as varied appeals as possible. **Really, fundamentally you are only supplying reasons why your performances will be enjoyed by your audiences.** Every one of these popular appeals you add will supply an additional selling point for **you.** Certainly no entertainer can afford to pass up opportunities to add audience appeal. That is what pays off, both in applause and fees.

At this moment Burling Hull's solution of the mind reading act, as he is now performing it, comes to mind. The thought transmission act is always interesting to an audience. Yet few performances are seen in which it is presented in the modern manner. Hull has done an excellent job of adding modern popular appeal.

To begin with he obtained the popularity associated with music, and its various appeals, by limiting the transmission to requests of specific musical numbers. He added sex-appeal and beauty by securing an attractive soprano. She is not merely a pretty girl but one with great charm and personality. Instead of a pianist, as in the old version, merely playing requested numbers whispered to the transmitter, this girl sings. And she sings very well.

To gain the advantage of the better musical background made available through the bands in the night clubs and hotels to which he caters, Hull has arranged the act in such a manner that these orchestras accompany the singer. Yet the band leader knows nothing whatever about the method of transmission.

By limiting each selection, except for the last one, to a few bars from each piece, he gains speed. And while the girl is singing Hull is getting his next request. This also cuts down on any

26

delays. Hull wears full dress and the girl is attired in an attractive evening gown.

This act has many appeals. The spectators have to like the act because it is made up of numbers of their own selection.

This brief outline illustrates one of the methods of adding popular appeal. Notice that the essentials of the act are conventional but that clever twists here and there have made it possible to incorporate many of the principles which foster public liking.

Music and rhythm have been added to the thought transmission act. The girl supplies youth, sex-appeal, personality and color. Through the songs, depending upon the specific numbers, are achieved harmony, melody, sentiment, nostalgia and romance. Comedy is accomplished through running comment on the part of the transmitter.

Careful attention has been given to timing, pointing, costumes, grooming, brevity and efficient pacing. Smoothness in the routine reflects efficient pacing, careful routining adds to a feeling of effortless skill, all accomplished by conscientious rehearsal. Other qualities include special material, punch, escape from the humdrum, unity, up-to-dateness—all building up to sure-fire reception.

CHAPTER FIVE

All of the foregoing, it will be realized, is merely preliminary to a detailed discussion as to how these qualities, repeatedly demonstrated as audience preferences, may be added to a magician's act or program. At this moment the list will seem long and complicated and perhaps too complex to be within the grasp of the average performer.

Because of the apparent difficulties presented in the adaptation of magic to popular presentation, it has been necessary to embark upon the long, detailed analysis of popular entertainment methods as represented by the foregoing. It is necessary because it is essential to convince the average magician of the utter necessity of adopting modern standards.

When it can be shown conclusively that **the entire entertainment industry**—movies, legitimate theatre, night clubs, etc.,— have based their entertainment product upon these fundamental principles of public response, the reason why the magic field should predicate its product upon the same appeals becomes obvious.

Shaping magic to these same standards is not too difficult. The objectives are plainly in sight. The biggest job is to find the methods that will accomplish the result, a job that the writer hopes will be accomplished through this work.

The same type of exploration as that made of the general entertainment field, with the few examples available in the magic field, plus the individual endeavors of the performers themselves should produce the desired answers.

Perhaps this work will be helpful in that direction.

To begin: Music. Instantly many will think of a waltz background while the performer indulges in a routine of digital calisthenics known as a manipulative moves. That positively is NOT what I mean. The way Malini used it comes nearer to the modern meaning:—

Malini would turn to the musicians and say pompously: "Professor. A tiny leedle valse." And then he would butt right in on the professor and go ahead with his performance, making it impossible for the professor to comply. He used this gag as a running tag throughout his performance, building up character and comedy.

Yet Malini's use is not exactly what I mean either. Music can set a mood, can establish a background, key a situation, reinforce a character. It can sympathetically interpret and color and add grace and rhythm, supplementary to, but invaluably building up, the primary interest.

Let me illustrate. In the opening of the final version of the International Magicians In Action show we made what I believe to be a very good example of establishment of audience contact. One of the first things a skillful performer does is to try to get on friendly terms with his audience. The same holds true of a production. If you get them to liking you in the beginning, you are well on your way to making them like almost anything you do.

We opened the show in the cocktail lounge of the magicians' club. This is impossible, of course, to anyone who has ever been a member of a magic club. But fortunately our audiences were laymen and were unfamiliar with the real character of most magicians' clubs. So we indulged in a little plausible poetic license.

Behind the bar was the comedian, acting as bartender and with the writer, impersonating the president of the club, in a few words setting the situation. The principals of the company, in modern evening dress, entered singly and in pairs and were individually introduced to the audience. Very casually, and with no emphasis upon the trick at all, the bartender did "Any Drink Called For" from the clear cocktail shaker as he asked the principals what they would have. The whole thing was casual and the cocktail trick was, in the parlance of the show business, "thrown away." Yet often the reviewers picked out that cocktail trick for favorable comment.

After the cocktails were poured, one of the characters suggested that everyone go out to a show and come back to the club afterward for a nightcap. Another character said that with all of that talent they should be able to put on their own show. Someone else mentioned that it would take a lot of money. Then another principal stepped forth and said he had an idea. He

29

picked up a champagne bucket and began picking money out of the air.

One by one the other members of the company started doing the same thing while the singer, with the orchestra accompanying her, went into "Pennies From Heaven."

With the exception of two or three who remained on the stage all of the principals went down into the audience and caught money from the air, occasionally handing a "sample" real half-dollar to one of the spectators.

It never failed to establish audience sympathy. This was partly because the performers were well-groomed, friendly and likeable in themselves and partly because of the mood established by the music. It was a familiar theme that was quite popular once and has retained its favor. The music brought nostalgia, romance, sentiment, rhythm, grace and many other qualities impossible to achieve without it. Part of the effect was because the music was familiar. A specially written number in this case could not have carried all of these qualities. That particular number established the whole routine and contributed heavily to selling it.

Now try to imagine what it would have lost without the musical background.

That is what I mean.

But, you say, that is all very well where you have a large company. What about the individual performer?

Clarence Slyter's drunk act is a fine example.

Slyter works silent. He staggers onstage in top hat and tails, quite obviously snorted to the eyes. There are some signs that he has been philandering around a bit. The whole routine is a series of happenings, perhaps true but more likely the imaginings of a befuddled rake, more and more bewildering to the hapless adventurer.

As a background, and fitting the various incidents, Slyter has a specially written score, cued to the running time of each trick in the routine, each number exactly fitting the space occupied by the trick itself and changing with the idea or mood. Such numbers as "Cocktails For Two," "Ann Boleyn," "Three o'Clock In the Morning," and the like are expertly interwoven in such a manner as to become part of the essential fabric of the act itself. Every bit of the music means something.

Practically any smart act, magical or otherwise, will show you how this is done and will furnish suggestions.

Here is another example from the International Magicians show. Murder In a Telephone Booth was a narrative number.

The narrator, as the King's counsellor, explains to the audience that a murder was committed in the Limehouse district in London. He further states that the audience has been selected as the jury and that a re-enactment of the crime will be done in order for them to reach a verdict.

Members of the company are introduced and they assume the make-up and costumes of the respective characters they are to impersonate. The judge is introduced and to a few bars from "Pomp and Circumstance," takes his place behind the bench, where he picks up a copy of the funnies and starts to read.

As the counsellor explains the crime the various characters enact it silently:—

The girl rushes into the telephone booth and hides while the orchestra plays "Pretty Baby." A tramp enters and saunters about while a few bars of "Brother Can You Spare a Dime" are played. He sees a cigarette stub. Music: "Smoke Gets In Your Eyes." And picks it up. Afterwards he crawls into a large packing case to spend the night. Music: "Sleep."

To the accompaniment of a mysterioso motif, the thug tip-toes towards the telephone booth, drawing a huge butcher knife, while the tramp watches him. After some business, the thug opens the phone booth door slightly and repeatedly stabs the screaming girl. As the thug sneaks away the orchestra plays the "Dead March."

The tramp cautiously leaves the box and finally gets up enough courage to look into the phone booth. He shudders while the music reverts to the "Dead March" again. Then he yells loudly for the police.

In the meantime, the principal playing the part of the bobby stands quietly at one side of the stage awaiting his cue. In spite of the fact that the tramp calls loudly and frantically the bobby takes his own sweet time to respond, and when he does every

31

movement is slow and deliberate. The music changes to "Running Wild."

He opens the phone booth door. It is empty. He shrugs, walks clear through and finally ambles down-stage in his puzzlement. When he takes off his helmet to scratch his head, gold blond hair falls down around his shoulders. It is the girl. (Music: "Pretty Baby.")

The counsellor protests and calls for the witness to explain the discrepancy in his story. The witness comes from the packing case and denies being the informant. When he takes off his beard and hat he is found to be the man who was originally playing the part of the judge.

The real witness calls from the back of the audience. He stands up, attired in full dress, and says the counsellor must be wrong, as he has been sitting in the audience all evening. With that the judge interrupts and says there need be no confusion as everyone has been accounted for. But with that, a horrible fact suddenly dawns upon him. With a cry of consternation he pulls the wig from his head saying, "My God, that makes me the murderer."

The counselor tears his hair. The telephone booth slams open and the policeman, attired in the girl's clothes, dashes wildly from the phone booth yelling, "What the hell's going on around here?"

There is a discordant chord from the orchestra. And a blackout.

The whole scene was enacted in a good-humored, tongue-in-the-cheek manner and the various music cues aided immeasurably in establishing the comedy treatment.

This kind of handling can add considerably to almost any type of **narrative** trick. It is fundamental, however, that the narrative be brief and to the point. **And vital to someone.** There must be no elaboration, no by-paths and no elocution. The murder routine took but 4½ minutes.

An example, parallel to the murder mystery, might be made of the linking ring trick, as a random selection. This adaptation is a comedy version of Charles Waller's lines as published in "For Magicians Only."

"An old, old feat of Eastern mysticism known to magicians

as "The Chinese Rings." (Music cue: "Chinatown, My China-town.") These are the rings. (Music cue: "I Got Rings on My Fingers.") Made of steel. (Music: "Anvil Chorus.") There are eight of them. (Music: The eight notes of the scale. Each played separately and distinctly.)

As the rings are handed out for examination, the orchestra goes into a fast Chinese motive. The time consumed in the exam-ination must be brief. It may even be dispensed with.

When the rings are all out: "All of the rings are in your possession." As the performer holds up his hands, showing them empty the orchestra plays a few bars of "I Got Plenty 'O Nuth-in'."

From here on individual routines vary and other music cues may be inserted to fit. However, this is made easier by having the orchestra go into a few bars of "Chinatown" every time a reference is made to the Chinese. Or when reference is made to "steel," a few bars from "The Anvil Chorus." Whenever a number of rings are counted, use an appropriate number of the notes of the scale.

Picking up the Waller lines again: "This trick is based on an old Chinese legend ("Chinatown") that tells of a famous warrior captured in battle (Orchestra: Deep discordant rumbling battle sounds), and condemned to die. ("Dead March.")

"Loaded and shackled with chains, he lie in prison. ("Pris-oner's Song.") On the night prior to the day fixed for his execu-tion ("It's Murder, He Says.") there appeared before him the Chinese God of Battle. (Elaborate fanfare.) Showing him how by magic to separate him chains link by kink, the Spirit vanished and left him to make his escape. ("Prisoner's Song.")

. . . "And yet, before your eyes, you see one ring gently melt through the other. . . . But you can't part the rings by force." ("Anvil Chorus.") "No. Back of this is a power more subtle than brute force." (Music: "Every Little Movement.")

"Softly, slowly as a Ghost passes through an open door ("Mysterioso"); so does one ring pass through the other."

"Just as a stone passes through water leaving but a ripple behind." ("Rustles of Spring.") Ad lib to fit your own routine.

Where the line: "The Marvelous Magic of the East" is spoken, bring in "Chinatown" again. "There is neither haste nor bustle.

("Please Go Way and Let Me Sleep.") "Just knock one ring into the other." ("Anvil Chorus.")

While doing the figures: For the clover: "Clover Blossoms." The rose, "Only a Rose," "Roses of Picardy" or "My Wild Irish Rose." The swing, "Rock-a-bye Baby." The ball, "After the Ball Was Over." Other titles will suggest themselves.

Additional comedy can be secured if you are good at facial expression. None of the figures look much like what they are called and the performer can have a dubious, somewhat skeptical expression on his face as he eyes each figure.

During the finale, when you are clashing and linking the rings into the usual jumble, go into "The Anvil Chorus" again.

When the rings are shown to be separate again at the end, count them off one by one. Meanwhile the orchestra plays the scale again, note by note, one note for each ring, in a descending sequence. The magician shrugs helplessly as the orchestra plays "I've Got Rings On My Fingers."

Just as the smart showman plans his productions to meet known audience preferences. And just as he incorporates as many of these surefire attractions into his script as possible. So also should the **kind** of material under each heading be selected to conform to public demand.

This is particularly true of the music incorporated in a routine.

The current issue of the Journal of the Acoustical Society of America (Oct. 1943), has a number of articles on the musical likes of several industrial groups. While the investigations upon which the reports are based are by no means complete, this preliminary report will be found of value to the entertainer in guiding him in making his selections.

Some of the results are surprising.

One report—that of the RCA Victor Division of the Radio Corporation of America—is based on a survey made of four selected groups located in Indianapolis, Camden, Chicago and Newark. The four groups included singers, stenographers, office workers and warehouse clerks and factory workers.

The ultimate results follow: All groups liked patriotic music. The singers and factory workers liked fast dance music, but the office workers and warehouse clerks did not. Surprisingly, the stenographers did not. All groups liked "Hit Parade" music. All groups liked Hawaiian music particularly, especially the factory workers. All groups liked humorous and novelty music.

The singers and office workers and warehouse clerks did not like semi-classical and standard music. The stenographers and factory workers did, but not strongly. All groups liked waltzes decidedly. The stenographers and factory workers did not dislike polkas and square dances, the others disliked them definitely.

All groups, with the exception of the singers, markedly disliked negro spirituals and blues. Even the singers' liking was only moderate. All groups liked marches.

Strangely, all groups expressed a strong liking for classical music, with the exception of the factory workers, who expressed liking for it but not a strong preference. Hillbilly and western music was liked only by the factory workers. The singers and the office workers and warehouse clerks expressed strong dislike. The stenographers were neutral.

The office workers and warehouse clerks were neutral on sacred and religious music. The factory workers liked this type more than the stenographers did. The singers expressed the strongest preference.

Now the above general results are not conclusive. They are preferences expressed by the workers in connection with music to be sent over the industrial public address systems at certain intervals during the working day. Under entertainment conditions the choices might change somewhat. Personally, I think the choices will change but little.

At least, this information gives definite clues for selecting music for an act.

One other point is important in connection with music: Ben Selvin, formerly recording director for a prominent recording company, gives the formula used by that company in preparing its arrangements for recording. He states, "The openings should be startling. The arrangements should include a change of color every twenty or thirty seconds. There should be a change of key between choruses and even sometimes in the middle of a chorus." He adds that a vocal refrain plus a fancy ending are almost "musts."

There are several very definite clues in connection with the arrangements for your music score.

Notice, also, how the usual formula for an act is repeated in the formula for arrangements: Attention-getting opening—varied pace—short numbers—variety in attack—novelty—and a punch closing.

CHAPTER SIX

Rhythm, even though allied to music, is a distinct appeal in itself. This is the blood tingling beat to which an audience responds while listening to popular bands. Similar audience reactions will be witnessed during the performances of tap dancers, rhythm singers, and exhibition drummers. The chief quality of one of the top-flight quartettes broadcasting over one of the networks is a keen stress on rhythm.

The rhythm doesn't necessarily have to be fast. As a matter of fact, the best recipe is to contrast the beats of various numbers.

In the International Magicians we combined a bit of nostalgia with sentiment and rhythm in our presentation of the floating ball. The number opened in one as a vibraharp solo with the soloist striking the opening chords slowly. As he launched into "Stardust" the curtains behind him parted very slowly, in tempo with the music, disclosing a lovely blonde girl in long flowing dress with a large silver ball in her hands. The background was a fulled silk curtain striped in pastel rainbow hues.

More as a dance made up of a series of poses, rather than a trick, the girl caused the ball to float about her in tempo with the music. Finally the ball slowly floated back towards her hands as the curtains started to close slowly. Just as the ball reached her hands she was cut from view and the soloist struck the last note. He took the bow as a soloist.

Manipulators have made use of this principle of rhythm, doing their moves in time with the music.

Marcia Adair does the mutilated parasol trick to the accompaniment of "A Pretty Girl Is Like a Melody." The entire routine is worked out in tempo with the music and the presentation which is silent is more of a series of slow dance movements. With a gracefully flowing red gown, the parasol and bag to match, this makes a very good sight number which has always registered well.

I've always thought that a comedy number could be worked out to some light accompaniment wherein the magician picked up, displayed and worked his apparatus in strict time with the music. The tempo should be brisk and the performer should definitely beat out the accents. Of course, brevity is important here as it is in practically all entertaining.

A punch could be added at the end where it would seem impossible that the performer could conclude in time with the music, but with a last-second frantic scramble he just makes it.

If you do a walk-on, rhythm can at least be added to the routine by entering briskly in step with the music.

Another method of adding rhythm is to use background accompaniment that is frankly rhythmic. Some of the smarter orchestral arrangements will supply this. Popular numbers or standard numbers in smart, modern rhythmic arrangements may be used. If you work with an accompanist only, rhythm can be stressed through the selection of the proper numbers alone, provided they are played with a good sense of modern rhythm preferences.

A cute walk-on motif, in dance tempo, could be used as the signature for the entrance of your girl assistant. It could be played every time she enters until she stops walking. Use of the same number would always identify this girl. But be sure she looks and acts and is costumed in keeping with the selection.

This idea of an identifying walk-on motif could be carried further to include all assistants, if more than one is used—a comedy number for the low comedy assistant, a kidding number for a good-looking straight chap, an elephantine type number for one who is inclined to be a bit fat. But keep them in strict tempo, the music with the step and the step with the music.

We used a lively march tempo, beaten out in military style by the drummer alone, to introduce our finale in the International Magicians show. After a few words stating that the audience has seen the magicians in action individually and that now they would be given an opportunity to see them in action collectively so that they might judge who is the greatest magician in the world, the drums broke into a military break. Immediately one of the magicians darted from the wings, the drum beating a march tempo, a megaphone to his mouth, shouting, "I'm the greatest magician in the world." He was followed at once by another, with a still larger megaphone, shouting the same thing. Still another and another and with each performer a larger megaphone and the same declaration, until the entire company was assembled across the stage.

At this moment the music changed to a fast rhythmic arrangement of "Marching Along Together." The curtains opened behind them, disclosing a stage full of apparatus—duck pans, bamboo frames, hats, bowl productions, flower productions, etc. And the magicians went to town with colorful silks, sailing cards, streamers, ringing alarm clocks, performing in three minutes an assortment of tricks which would normally take an hour and a half to do. The stage was a three-ring circus of magic, motion, color, action and rhythm.

While it has no bearing on this rhythm idea, I may as well give you a full description of this finale.

At the height of the action on the stage, with the quacking of ducks, cackling of chickens, ringing of bells, with the stage littered in silks, the magicians knee-deep in serpentine, a loud shot is heard off-stage. An attractive girl, dressed in a bunny costume and carrying a silk hat, dashes to center stage. Frozen in the positions they were in when the shot was fired, all cry, "Well. Who are you?"

The girl: "I'm the rabbit. And I don't care who is the greatest magician in the world." Whereupon she plunges her hand into the hat and brings forth . . . a magician, in the form of a doll in full dress with silk topper. Curtain.

As a further suggestion in connection with rhythm, a certain type of magician might be able to deliver his lines in rhythm. I don't mean verse. Some of the quartettes on the air do their songs in this manner, more in a rhythmic talking style than singing.

Now on the subject of youth and sex-appeal:

It is best of course if the performer can conduct himself in a youthful manner—I mean youthful in contrast with the deliberateness and slowly considered movements of middle age. For those who are not youthful, make-up will help, also a youthful slant to their thinking. Proper costuming will add to an illusion of youth, as well.

But if the performer himself is not youthful, he can at least secure youthful assistants. What has been said about a male performer of middle age holds true as well of a female assistant in the same age brackets. If she has youthful contours, dresses and acts in a youthful manner, is made up to look young and animated, she can gain the desired effect if she goes at it with intelligence and good taste.

However, the best solution is to use young-looking assistants of both sexes.

Youth is an undeniable selling point.

Now how does one go about stressing sex-appeal in female assistants without becoming vulgar? Fundamentally, it is a matter of an extremely discriminating sense of good taste. The costumes may be a bit brief, a bit snug to reveal contours, a bit flattering to both complexion and figure. Remember, a long gown properly designed can carry more sex-appeal than a brief costume without the subtle suggestions possible in the longer gown. Stress should be laid on feminine touches, an ornament here, a bit of ribbon there, a bit of flirting with the eyes, a tantalizing smile.

There are so many ways that sex-appeal may be added to the show without becoming a liability, and so many more ways that clumsy attempts to add sex-appeal will ruin the whole thing, that it is almost impossible to set down general rules.

But a bit of study given to the way this is done in the movies— angles, expressions, emphasis here and there, color, design, cut, coiffure, even movements—extended study will reveal more of specific value, with a definite objective in mind, than a thousand generalizations.

A study of methods of emphasizing sex-appeal is a whole career in itself as will become instantly clear when it is realized to what ends the films have gone in glamorizing hundreds of quite ordinary girls. Glamour, you know, is merely a name for deliberately contrived sex-appeal.

Probably that dictionary definition of sex as "the character of being male or female" more clearly emphasizes the exact shade of meaning intended here. Any expedient that awakens a response to the fact that a person is male or female, in our present sense, particularly female, will build up sex-appeal. The appeal must be subtle and indirect. This is because numerous inhibitions and complexes, partly because of our training and partly through inherited characteristics, cause us to withdraw from any such suggestion which is forthright, frank or undisguised.

This is an important point, this necessity of being indirect in this appeal. The girl must seem totally unconscious of her attraction. She must seem wholly unaware that her costume, the accentuating features, her effeminateness, mannerisms and the like are designed to appeal in this manner.

Why the indirect appeal is stronger with the more intelligent type is again psychological, based on reasons which are too involved for discussion here. But the basic rule of subtility cannot be ignored without disaster.

CHAPTER SEVEN

The most valuable single product of th show business today is that quality known as personality. That set of characteristics, qualities, mannerisms which distinguishes and characterizes a person as an unique individual constitutes a complex commodity known as his personality.

Whether the attraction is a motion picture, a stage production, the floor show in a night club or a hotel dining room, a contest or any of the numerous diversions people seek for entertainment, the big attraction is the star. Hard-headed business men have finally found, via the indisputable logic of the box office total, that **people are more interested in people than in any other single thing**.

In order of importance general appeal responds first to the allure of outstanding personages, second to the reasons why people do things and third to the things people do.

Now how does this star become a personality?

There is more in it than just the manner in which a man tells a story. There is more than the expertness with which a girl may dance. More than the way an actor or actress interprets a line. Or in the facial expression he may contrive to accompany a single situation.

Underlying it all is an almost indefinable thing called personality.

Take a few outstanding stars whose attraction to the public has been proven—Al Jolson, Ed Wynn, Clark Gable, Shirley Temple, Mickey Rooney, Bette Davis, Robert Taylor, Bing Crosby, Greer Garson, Paulette Goddard or any others. This list includes singers, comedians, actors, child stars, dramatic stars. Each of them has various talents, in varying degrees, some surpassing others in certain qualities and in turn being surpassed in other characteristics. At first it would seem that none of them has anything in common except for the fact that they are in the show business.

But that isn't quite true.

First of all, every one of them is a distinct individual. No one else on earth is exactly like any one of them. In addition each

42

has individual personal characteristics. Each has a distinctly individual appearance.

Each has an individual set of tastes, likes and dislikes, preferences, attitudes towards others, method of dress, manner of speaking, physical carriage and many other numerous distinguishing features.

To his work each brings some special quality in a superlative degree. In Jolson's case there are many singers whose voices are far better—in this writer's opinion, as an example, Bing Crosby. But there are many individualizing touches to Jolson's delivery of a song as there are to Crosby's.

Putting all of Jolson's distinguishing qualities together—and I mean ALL—there is possible only one result. That result is distinctly Al Jolson. The same holds true of Crosby, Rooney, Shirley Temple as she was at the height of her career, Miss Goddard, Miss Garson and any of the others. Or, for that matter, any of the other stars who have caught the public fancy from Jack Dempsey and Babe Ruth to Ethel Waters.

So the one thing ALL of these people have in common is their distinct individuality.

If every person on earth looked like every other person and did the same things, saying the same words with the same inflections, there would be no way of distinguishing one from the other. The components which make you the individual you are are entirely contained in the variations you employ—in mannerisms, thoughts, attitudes, viewpoints, behavior, appearance, grooming, work, ambitions, beliefs, etc.—from the normal standard.

To achieve distinct individuality as a magician it is necessary that you be distinguished from the rank and file. The distinguishing marks are entirely due to the combination of features which is exclusively your own. If this combination is pleasing to others, you have a pleasing personality. If this combination is **superlatively** pleasing, you are on your way to stardom. All that remains is to contrive a way to advertise to the greatest number of people that you have this combination.

Dale Carnegie has written a book which should be an essential in every entertainer's library. You probably know the title of that book is "How To Win Friends and Influence People." In this book he states that the fundamentals of winning friends are four: (1) Don't criticize others; (2) Try to understand people; (3) Look for the good points in others and express them; and (4) Think in terms of the other fellow's point of view.

He also gives six ways to make people like you. The general rules are: (1) Become genuinely interested in other people; (2) Smile; (3) Remember people's names; (4) Be a good listener and encourage others to talk about themselves; (5) Talk in terms of the other person's interests; and (6) Sincerely, make the other person feel important.

There is a liberal education in improved personal relations within the two covers of that work. Get it by all means.

What aspects does any of these entertainers present to his audiences? What aspects does any magician present to his audiences?

They must be discernible through the five senses. Three of these are rarely employed by a spectator, those of taste, feel and smell. That leaves the impression created through what is seen and heard.

To the spectator's sight the magician presents several aspects. (1) A definite personality—pleasing, funny, stodgy, ponderous, pompous. The list is limitless. (2) A definite complexion—light, dark, medium, dirty, clean. (3) A costume—conventional or unconventional, appropriate or inappropriate. (4) The properties with which he works—tasteful, gaudy, ordinary, unusual, well-cared-for or neglected, etc. (5) A carriage—upright, sloppy, stooped, slender, ponderous, and so on. (6) Tempo—jerky, smooth, slow, moderate. (7) An approach—hesitant, confidant, cocky, frightened, nervous.

A more detailed analysis should be made of the external aspects of several of the prominent stars, preferably those much above any magician in prominence. Compare these features with an equally detailed analysis of your own. Try to discover the outstanding advantages this star, or these stars, possess. Then endeavor to acquire for yourself similar advantages for public reception.

If a magician does a talking routine, he has several sound effects at his disposal. (1) Volume—a loud, medium or soft voice. (2) Pitch—high, medium or low. (3) Quality—raspy, vibrant or mellow. (4) Articulation—precise, clear or mumbled. (5) Delivery—fast, jerky, smooth, slow, halting, drawling, etc. (6) Method of delivery—extemporaneous, studied, timed, pointed, careless.

In addition to the qualities of the voice and the method of speaking, the entertainer must consider the material he is uttering. But the material can be no better than the interpretation of the performer delivering it. Thus we have a new quality which, as far as the voice goes, is based on tonal modulation, variety in the delivery tempo and the mind behind the performer.

At this point, interpretation, the senses of sight and hearing combine to receive the effect. Proper reception is based partly upon the words heard, the facial and bodily expressions seen and the meaning sensed.

Even the silent act appeals to the two principal senses.

There is one more influencing factor that goes to make up the individuality of an entertainer, even a magician. This is the material used. Three essential factors constitute this material— the things seen, the things heard and the meaning conveyed.

The writer has said before that if every performer looked and performed alike, and used the same material, there would be nothing to distinguish one from the other. The way to gain individuality, then, is to MAKE YOUR PERFORMANCE DIFFERENT FROM THE USUAL. But this must be consistent with your abilities, personality, education.

The way to gain superlative individuality which will please your audiences is to make this difference SUPERLATIVE in the direction of favorable audience reception.

Starting with material: It is best to use effects and lines that are exclusively your own. Have the production professionally prepared. You can at least add something of your own in the way of a twist to the effects, delivery, lines, angle of approach, style or any of the other numerous phases. SOMETHING MUST BE DIFFERENT, BE INDIVIDUAL TO YOU, ABOUT THE MATERIAL AND DELIVERY OR YOU FAIL TO ESTABLISH INDIVIDUAL IDENTITY AT THE FUNDAMENTAL.

Give considerable attention to your costume. Regardless of what you wear—conventional business suit, full dress, dinner coat, character costume—see if there is not some way that you can achieve a distinctive identification. This must mean you and no one else.

Consider the various optical aspects you can present. Search for individuality opportunities, some way of identifying yourself from the rank and file. BUT KEEP THESE IDENTIFICATIONS CONSISTENT AND IN CHARACTER WITH YOU AND YOUR ACT.

The audible aspects include volume, pitch, quality, articulation, delivery, modulation, tempo, interpretation. Somewhere there is a combination of these factors which will be pleasing to your spectators and consistent with yourself. Add these to your list of distinguishing tags.

Never lose sight of the fact, in adopting these identifying mark, that they must be PLEASING TO THE SPECTATORS. No matter how distinctly you identify yourself, if the net result is not a favorable impression on your audience, you have failed. PLEASING THE SPECTATOR IS INDISPENSIBLE.

Experienced theatre men, particularly from the production field, can give you basic assistance in audience appeal. But the sure way of discovering what pleases an audience and what does not is in trying it ON THE AUDIENCE YOURSELF. You will find out unmistakably.

Discover the most effective numbers in your program. Then see if you can find more effective substitutions for those items which make the least impression. By a continuing process, always attacking the weaker numbers, you gradually build up your routine. Perhaps, eventually, even the numbers you find strongest now will be eliminated.

But all the time, regardless of this basic material, TRY TO GIVE EVERYTHING SOMETHING INDIVIDUAL AND EX-CLUSIVELY YOUR OWN.

When your style is individual—style is made up of the optical and audible aspects mentioned before—and your material is individual, you as a performer are an easily identified, distinctive performer. This is expressed personality.

If you should take the time to analyze outstanding entertainers such as Bob Hope, Fred Allen, Jack Benny and others, even some of the magicians, although NONE OF THEM begin to approach the big stars of the theatre in audience appeal, you will find each is equipped with an **exclusive** set of distinctive identifying qualities which have strong appeal to the public. And none is like the other IN ANY WAY.

Make no mistake. The material itself, while important, **is purely secondary.** First is a tremendously magnetic personality. Take the material you have, these tricks you do. Spend every minute you can on it until you can do it in your sleep, as far as the operative part is concerned. Then forget the material as something to do in front of an audience.

You have only one thing to do in front of an audience—and that is TO SELL YOURSELF. Sell yourself every second of every minute you are in front of an audience. Work at it; sweat at it. Drive it home. Make them know it. You are not a magician. Forget that stuff. You're an entertainer.

Make them like you better than your magic. Make them like you so much they would even pay to hear you sing, or tell stories. Make them want to witness your entertainment RE-GARDLESS OF WHAT YOU DO.

Hammer at it. Drive at it. Dig at it. Me, **Me, ME.** Think: "I've got to sell 'em **me.** I've got to make them know that **I** am the important thing." Forget what a good trick the linking rings or the cut rope or the egg bag is.

Let them have all of the **you** you can give them.

You haven't many minutes to do it in these days. But you must do it. Or the next time they won't ask for you. They won't want **you.** They'll want the tricks. And if they want the tricks, any magician will do—just any one. What do they care who the guy is? They want to see the tricks.

It's just as easy as pushing a baby carriage. All you have to know is which end to push. Maybe that's why it took longer for Father's Day to click than Mother's Day.

Push the **man** doing the tricks. Not the tricks.

This idea of selling yourself has been used to advantage by all kinds of salesmen—automobiles, battleships, rat traps. If you sell them on you, they won't care what kind of rat trap you sell. It's the man they're doing business with. Not the Hoover vacuum cleaner.

The minute you stop selling yourself in the entertainment field and start selling your goods instead, that very minute you are starting to pick your own pocket. Instead of creating a set-up for yourself, you are creating a set-up for the kind of goods you sell. Then somebody else can get the order. He sells the same thing.

And if they can get what they want from the other fellow a little cheaper, or more for their money, they'll buy from him. That's why you must sell **the man,** the entertainer as an individual, instead of the kind of entertainment. The only time they can get **you,** at **your** price, is to buy from **you.**

Make your personality what they want. The only thing you should be concerned with is in impressing them with yourself.

Here's looking at YOU.

CHAPTER EIGHT

Color is in keeping with certain types of acts and not in keeping with others. There is nothing more out of character than a stoutish man in business suit pulling yards and yards of silk, in effeminate pastel shades, from a hat or a box or a tube.

In Ade Duval's act, which has been titled Rhapsody In Silk, during which the stage becomes covered with a profusion of specially designed silks in a profusion of colors, it is in character. But those colors are distinctively chosen.

In the costumes of girl assistants, feminine tints are in good character, if handled with a discriminating eye to color harmony and contrast. But the male assistant, if attired in color, should prevail in the stronger hues.

This color idea must be handled with care. Everything that has color should be selected to some predominating key. Just mere splashes of indiscriminate heterogeneous pastel shades are usually gaudy, blatant and very poor taste.

Color should not be acquired at random, selected just because some individual silk appeals to the performer, without regard to colors that are to be used with it, or disregarding other groups of colors. Usually color should be selected with great care, in not too great a profusion, by someone capable of combining colors in good harmony.

If the colors are to be seen in artificial light they should be selected with the warming influence of artificial light in mind. A stage designer usually makes his selections from a pallette somewhat colder than what the ultimate appearance is to be, just because of the warming effect of artificial light.

Even the whitest illumination is not really white. It is deficient in certain cold ranges. The result is that pale yellows, oranges, pinks and certain reds "wash out," while the tints of green and blue become grayed.

Under colored illumination such as green, blue or red, unbelievable changes take place. Red light turns blue black and red white. Blue light causes red to appear as black or dark gray, while blue seems white.

It is almost impossible to get such shades as lavender under white light, while red or blue light causes the violet hues to appear, respectively, red or blue, whichever the illumination.

Just because you are a magician, it is not necessary to use the conventional variegated colors. If the character of your routine is such that silks are in keeping, have the colors in keeping with the type of act. Perhaps a great many acts now using silks would be better off without them.

While color is desirable and pleasing to the public, it is not absolutely essential. It is highly undesirable if it is out of character with the routine. Can you imagine, as an example, Bob Hope, or Bing Crosby, or Jack Benny, or Al Jolson, ringing in effeminate variegated pastel shades, except for a laugh?

The word, "harmony," has a great many meanings as applied to the show business. It really means the quality of being pleasing to the senses, to hearing, to sight, to the feelings. It means an accord in feeling, action or manner. It carries with it a sense of completeness and perfection resulting from diversity in unity, orderliness, agreement in relating the various parts of the whole.

It not only means a satisfactory balance in color. But it means also a harmonious balance of the whole act. It means that the character of the performer, his costume, the properties, the music the rhythm and tempo, the delivery, the grooming—all components—complement, reinforce, add contrast, add strength, blend tastefully into a completely satisfying entity.

Good taste and a sense of the fitness of things are invaluable in achieving complete harmony.

Occasionally a bit of romance may be integrated into the entertainment. It may come as the result of a song, a musical number, or through the narrative accompanying a trick. There is a great difference between romance and dripping sentimentalism. Heroic self-sacrifice, the quest for an ideal, or devotion to a person or a cause are often much more romantic than a mere love affair. This quality, if sought, and if in keeping with the character of the act, must be handled with a great deal of discretion or it can become nauseating.

Your appeals to sentiment need not necessarily be direct. Often it can be brought in by implication. The songs of Al Jolson such as "Mammy," and love for home, or the South supply sentiment. Most of Bing Crosby's songs bring in sentiment of one kind or another. Although many people mistake a biological urge for sentiment, it is too narrow a meaning.

Sentiment is emotional. It is awakened by things that seem to have worth like mother love, love of country, sacrifice and the long list of things we have been taught to believe are good. It is a feeling of response in the soul.

But if it becomes maudlin, it does terrific damage.

One example of a sentiment appeal was the use we made of Marilyn Miller's old number, "Easter Parade," in the International Magicians show. It was used as the background when the entire company tore tissue squares and converted them to a variety of hats.

A good example of romance appeal was another number we built up with the doll house illusion.

The soprano, a young girl, was singing "Castle of Dreams" from "Irene." After the first chorus the curtains behind her parted, disclosing a miniature replica of a cottage with the boy friend beckoning to her. When she asked him what it was, he told her it was a model of a love nest he was going to have built just for her. Turning the house around, he showed her the windows from which she would hang the laundry. Around facing the front again, he showed her the inside and brought forth the upper floor to show her the furniture. Meanwhile the girl was cooing with delight.

Backgrounding the dialogue were still the strains of the song the girl had been singing. The boy showed her the front door and where the card would announce, "Mr. and Mrs." Then, with just a bit of worry, the girl asked if there ever had been another girl in his life. He protested, "No," very strongly, whereupon the doll house opened and a sophisticated-looking gal in red dress stood up and said dryly, "The same old line, eh, Daddy?" Blackout.

Romance can be worked into a magic routine, but it must be done intelligently. Just a mere romantic narrative to accompany some trick done with a red box or a flock of purple silk scarfs won't do. Patter lines positively are corny, regardless of the subject, unless done as broad comedy, kidding the performer himself.

51

However, two good looking young people could doubtless develop a cute courtship number. To make it interesting, there must be a bit of conflict, perhaps a rival for the girl's hand, or reluctance on her part. Through some trick—I mean a trick from a magician's point of view—he overcomes the girl's objections and she falls in his arms.

Such an idea might be built up from the following: The girl walks by and the magician tips his hat and takes from it a bouquet which he hands to her. She looks at it indignantly, changes it to a cabbage which she hands back to him. He reaches in the air and produces a cigarette. Intrigued, the girl watches him. He produces a box of matches, extracts one, throws the box in the air and scratches the match, after which he lights his cigarette. He makes a pass at his cigarette and it vanishes, appearing in the girl's mouth. She takes it from her mouth, indignantly, throws it down, but immediately finds another in her hand. She does it again and again, while the boy watches her laughing. Finally, in desperation she appeals to him. He causes it to vanish and reappear in his own hands.

Frankly intrigued now, the girl watches him as he materializes a single rose and offers it to her. She shakes her head and pantomimes that the rose is the wrong color. He passes his hand over it. Still not right. Again. This time the color pleases her and she smiles. He kisses the rose, tosses it in the air and it reappears on her dress or in her hair.

Now he produces a scarf which he throws around her shoulders or ties around her head. Then he produces a bottle and a glass and pours a drink of wine. He hands it to her, but as she touches it she shakes her head naughty-naughty and it changes to milk, which she immediately transforms to a can of evaporated milk and carefully stows into her bag.

Now he has a baby chick in his hand which he cuddles within his cupped palms. The girl leans close to look and the boy kisses her. She seems to like it but draws away like a good little girl. He produces a dollar bill from the air, another and another. She comes closer as he produces the money, takes his arm. His arm slips around her as she watches in delight. Finally, he brings forth a wallet into which he carefully shows the money and prudently puts it into his pocket.

52

He produces a parasol, hands it to the girl, links her arm in his, plucks a cigar from the air and walks off with the girl. As they reach the exit, the girl pulls his arm around her and, her arm free, deftly extracts the wallet from the pocket of the blissfully ignorant boy.

For music a series of numbers immediately suggest themselves. When the girl enters: "A Pretty Girl Is Like a Melody." When he produces the bouquet: "Give Me One Dozen Roses." When he produces the cigarette: "Smoke Gets In Your Eyes." When he materializes the single rose: "Only a Rose," or "Roses In Picardy." When he produces the bottle: "Sweet Adeline." When she changes the wine to milk: a rube number. When he kisses her: "Just a Little Love a Little Kiss."

During the money production: "Pennies From Heaven." And at the end: "'Love Is the Grandest Thing."

The above is not an act. It is merely the SUGGESTION for an act. Between the writing of that outline and the performance of the entertaining act lie multitudes of details. The various properties must be secured, each PERFECTLY suited to this routine. The various moves, business, actions and reactions must be interconnected and interrelated to a routine. Costumes must be selected. Endless rehearsals must be held. All excess must be trimmed out, until finally a satisfactory act seems to have been developed. Then a musical score is written, timed perfectly with the act.

After that there must be endless rehearsals until the whole thing becomes almost second nature, until it can be done subconsciously.

The act as it will finally be evolved may resemble the original synopsis very little. In fact, if many added, better and more original ideas have not been developed, as attention is given to specific details, it is almost certain that you have failed. Few finished routines are the same as the original idea. Thought plus an idea are basic components of a good entertaining routine. An idea, alone, is seldom more than an initial sign-post.

We now come to nostalgia, that longing for home and the things of the happy past. Certainly there is no better way of bringing in this old reliable than through music. Hundreds of hit tunes of past years are capable of reawakening memories of people, places, episodes and the like.

For this purpose a magician might well team-up with a singer and do his routine in conjunction with a routine of songs. Of course, the material used should be appropriate to the songs selected. If a singer isn't available, a pianist will do quite as well. A combination of a good pianist, with the magician working within the curve of a grand piano, might be a definitely pleasing novelty. Certainly, many audience appeals are possible.

Nostalgic comedy is inherent in a routine which might burlesque the old-fashioned "Professor." This burlesque need not be too broad, and neither need it be far removed from the conventional performance of magic as witnessed even today.

CHAPTER NINE

Timing and pointing are two very closely related tools of the expert showman. Without a good sense of these two essentials, it is almost impossible to be a good entertainer. They are perhaps the two most important expedients in that most difficult of all branches of the show business, comedy.

Perfect examples of timing and pointing are available weekly to everyone through the performances of the top radio comics such as Bob Hope, Edgar Bergen, Jack Benny, Fred Allen and many others. Notice the tempo of delivery, the pauses, the emphasis, the slowing down of tempo as a point is about to be reached and the longer pause just before the carefully timed delivery of the punch line. This is not extemporaneous. It is the most deliberately studied arrangement in the program.

Part of it rests in conveying the situation leading up to the gag. The slightly slower tempo is to set up the exact set of conditions unmistakably, clearly, to the spectators. The pause, often, is psychological, to tease attention and anticipation so that the surprise or devastating punch will hit the auditor with full impact.

Pointing indicates, or shows, the objective. Timing has to do with EMPHASIZING that objective. Pointing tells you, "This is it." Timing says, "Look how important it is."

Timing might be defined, in this sense, as the deliberate control or regulation of tempo as to speech, movement or business, selecting and spacing time, as portions of duration, in such a manner as to accomplish a definite objective unmistakably. That objective might be to secure understanding clearly, to add surprise, to develop punch, to add meaning, to build up to a climax, to build up suspense, provoke anticipation or any of the multitudinous objectives possible in public entertainment.

A familiar example of timing is the gradual ritard a singer uses, if he is a good showman, as he approaches the end of his number. Notice how he gradually slows the tempo, more and more, as he comes to the climax of the song, building it up to a smash finish.

The writer has always gotten a good reception for his presentation of the razor blade trick. It is almost entirely a matter of build up and suspense through timing.

Because in the theatre it is almost impossible to distinguish the razor blades, particularly from the rear seats and the balcony in a large house, it was found necessary to prelude the routine with the explanation that "These are razor blades." Except for these words, and the piano solo—even when an orchestra was available—background of Rachmaninoff's "Prelude In C-Sharp Minor," painstakingly timed to the routine, the presentation is silent.

With no lighting, except for a white spotlight, the package of razor blades is exhibited. The explanation is given, after which each blade is unwrapped and shown individually. Just once during this unwrapping I seem to cut myself accidentally. It is a minor cut of no consequence and the appearance is given that the performer is trying to cover his awkwardness, even though bothered a bit by the cut. Once only, a blade is shown to be sharp by slicing a piece of paper.

The emphasis is on unwrapping the blades and showing each individually. This is done with some deliberateness. Then, one at a time, in a tempo just a bit slower, the blades are dipped in a glass of water and thus moistened are placed within the mouth.

A sip is taken from the glass after the last blade is out of sight and simultaneously a spool of thread is taken from the pocket.

With great care and deliberation a length of white thread is unreeled from the spool and broken off. This is folded and also placed in the mouth. There is a pause of approximately ten seconds, without any movement on the part of the performer. Then he slowly reaches towards his mouth.

The end of the thread is seized and one blade is brought forth. On the first of the final seven grand chords in the Prelude the second blade is brought into view. The chords, impressive, magnificent, lifting, gradually ritard slower and slower—and with each chord a blade appears—until with the final chord the last blade is revealed. And the performer grasps the free end of the thread, holding the flashing blades dangling in front of him. And slowly bows, even as the chords are still echoing.

56

I am aware that amateur magicians criticize me severely because they believe I take too much time with this trick. But the criticisms of amateur magicians, generally, are valueless. As a matter of fact there is invariably more destructive criticism from an amateur magician, in discussing almost any performance of magic, than there is constructive. There is a psychological reason for this, going back into the critic's ego.

So it is best not to listen to the volunteer critic, unless one has reason to know that his taste is sound and his advice valuable.

I have performed this trick hundreds of times in hundreds of different ways. The blades have been used both wrapped and unwrapped. They have been placed in the mouth in a bunch and singly. The tempo has been varied, slow and fast and combinations of both. I've tried it with and without patter. It has been tried with and without music. Other musical settings have been used with it.

That routine has been developed on a basis of AUDIENCE RESPONSE. It is the culmination of years of experiment in selling the trick to the public. For ME, it is the most effective method of presentation. That is why I use it.

Now I don't particularly enjoy performing the razor blade trick. It is the one trick in my repertoire I least enjoy doing. I made this statement to a chap one time, and he immediately rushed into print with the statement that I said it was the least effective trick I did. He, of course, didn't understand me and took me to task because in his opinion it was the most effective thing I did.

To set matters right: I least enjoy doing that trick. But I do it because it receives the STRONGEST RECEPTION OF ANYTHING I DO. I know it is one of my best audience registrations. That's why I do it. That's why, as I've often said, a magician should not necessarily select the tricks he likes to do best. He should select those the AUDIENCE likes best.

The entire impression is made through timing.

Another example of timing comes from a specially written finish for a low comedy magic act we used in the International Magicians. In this act nothing the comedy magician tried came out the way he intended it to. But instead of taking the blame for the failure, every expression of the performer plainly showed that he blamed his poor, stupid, silent low-comedy assistant.

As his final number the curtains opened and two added assistants were seen standing on either side of the piece of illusion apparatus known as The Disembodied Princess. After some by-play, the magician entices his assistant into the cabinet and the doors are closed after which the usual blades are slid through, trisecting the hapless helper.

Now comes the illustration in timing:

The magician opens the door, disclosing the helper's legs. He opens the upper door, showing the head. Then he swings open the front middle door and likewise opens the door at the rear. The assistant has no middle. His body is missing from thigh to neck.

Without any further ado, satisfaction on his face, he picks up his hat and starts for the left downstage wings, not even looking back at the illusion.

One of the assistants yells, "Hey. Aren't you going to put him together again?"

The magician continues, unanswering, until he reaches a position about four steps from the exit. Then he turns and asks, "What the hell do you think I am?" He turns and takes three steps further, bringing him about one step from the wings.

Then he turns again and adds, "A magician?"

He claps on his hat and steps out of sight.

Curtain.

Pointing is emphasizing and accenting, by word and action, in such a manner that the material is aimed at a particular effect. It is the directing of all effort towards a specific objective upon which the entertainer desires to fix attention with special importance. It is a matter of interpretation, resembling misdirection, under which classification misdirection really belongs. Misdirection is a minor division under the heading of pointing.

The mere recitation of patter is not pointing. The delivery of lines, with interpretation, facial expression, gestures and other accentuation, in such manner that attention is directed to a specific end, is pointing.

An example of pointing is shown in the substitution trunk routine we developed for the International Magicians.

The curtain opens to disclose a lazy Mexican, lying flat on his back, head comfortably cradled in his arms, hat over his face, thoroughly partaking of his siesta. Behind him is the adobe wall and one corner of the hacienda. To one side, tired and dejected, may be seen the drooping form of his long suffering spouse, sitting patiently atop a large trunk.

Finally the girl says, "If we do not be moving right away, we will never get thees trunk to Mexico City."

From beneath the hat: "I cannot walk another step until I have rested. I am very tired."

"You are very lazy," the girl exclaims indignantly. "It is I who have carried thees trunk all the way from Juarez. And I am not tired."

"You have not the brains to be tired—so I have to be tired for you."

The girl says scornfully, "Oh, I have not the brains, eh? I have the brains to ask two dollar for to carry thees trunk."

The man gets to one elbow. "Si, si, muchacha. But I have the brains to collect the money." He waves the bills in the air nonchalantly.

The girl grabs at the money, saying, "Here. That is mine."

But without exerting undue energy, the man pulls the bills out of reach. "Don't ever try a trick like that again. If I am on my feet now, I teach you a lesson.—Remind me to beat you sometime when I am stand up." He settles back to sleep again.

At this juncture four men tourists enter and one of them says, "Could you tell us the direction to Mexico City?"

Pointing with his foot, but otherwise unmoving, the Mexican says, "It is six kilometer that way."

When one of the men remarks, "Those are the laziest instructions I ever heard," another says to the Mexican, "If you do a lazier trick than that I'll give you a dollar."

Languidly the Mexican rolls over so that his pocket is uppermost and says, "Put the money in my pocket and I show you."

Having received the money, the Mexican gets to his feet reluctantly and shuffles lazily over to prop himself comfortably against the proscenium arch. Then he directs his wife to show the trunk to the men. While this is being done, incidentally showing the trunk as well to the audience, the Mexican dozes peacefully. But a large cut-out caricature of a head pops up over the top of the adobe wall and ducks out of sight again.

Presently it returns, but accompanied by two others. They are disreputable-looking Mexicans with an overwhelming curiosity directed towards the trunk.

Suddenly the dozing Mexican whips out a revolver and lets fly at the eaves-droppers. They fall behind the wall.

One of the tourists cries, "Who's that?"

"Oh," says the Mexican with a shrug, indifferently, "They are my brothers. All the time they try to steal this trick."

At this juncture a lovely girl in shorts enters and is greeted by the tourists. The Mexican takes one look at her and says to his wife, "Ramona. You go home."

Ramona flashes a vengeful look at the other girl, but dutifully starts off. As she reaches the wings she stops and says, "Pancho. Someday I kick the hell out of you." But she leaves.

Under the Mexican's direction the girl is placed in the sack and into the trunk. The trunk is roped and locked after which a sort of a tent-like canopy is held over the trunk by the four men.

Still leaning against the proscenium, Pancho says, "You think Pancho is a very lazy guy, no? Well, I am now going to show you the fastest trick in the world."

One of men says, "Oh, yeah?"

Pancho takes out a cigarette, calmly lights it. He blows out the match, apathetically. "I show you I move pretty damn quick. WATCH!"

With that he suddenly galvanizes into action. He leaps across the stage. He dives into the canopy. Almost in the same instant the four men jerk the canopy away from the trunk. But the girl, in bewilderment, dashes forward crying, "Where's Pancho?"

Ultimately, after the trunk has been opened and the sack has been untied, Pancho, of course, is found sitting comfortably inside the trunk, smoking the cigarette.

Curtain

As is well-known, the substitution trunk is particularly one of great speed. Miss Adair and myself had so routined every movement, economizing time and eliminating movements—even to the point that I dived directly into the trunk from the outside of the canopy, that we were out of sight only two-fifths of a second, by repeated timings with stop watch.

To emphasize this speed the lines and action were all pointed constantly to the contrast of the extremely lazy magician and the consequently unexpectedly sensational speed which featured the trick. The punch was made stronger by this contrast.

As an example of pointing, this routine was selected because the pointing is so clear and unmistakable. But the majority of such examples are much more subtle and less direct, as employed usually in professional entertaining.

In the case of the finale to the comedy act, outlined previously, the magician was building up to the eventual fate of his low-comedy assistant being left without his middle, in showing his increasing disgust with the clumsiness of his assistant throughout the earlier part of the act. This was definitely pointing to the ultimate laugh climax, building up a reason for the assistant's ultimate finale predicament and the magician's ultimate revenge.

Pointing is the stressing of all factors to a definite aim, stressing in every way attention on the desired end and lightening the emphasis on any distracting by-path. There should not be a multitude of objectives. Each trick to be most effective should concentrate on one single climax.

Such climaxes might be danger, comedy smash, surprise, impossibility, incongruity, action, sentiment or any other similar conceivable aim.

For a danger climax stress is laid on the factors contributing the danger. Often this may be done through little subtle touches such as the feigned accidental cut mentioned in the presentation of the razor trick.

In the case of the comedy, emphasis should be put on those factors which will strengthen the comedy point, whichever type of comedy may be utilized. Everything which will distract from this ultimate goal should be subordinated or eliminated.

For a surprise climax, stress should be placed on those factors which will lead away from a premature denouement. All attention should be given to insure no betraying clues.

Obviously the most effective pointing would accent the logic and reasonableness of something else when a climax of impossibility or incongruity is desired, with equal effort devoted to making what the ultimate result is to be seem entirely out of the realm of plausibility or reasonableness.

Where emotional responses are desired all of the possibilities of making the spectator place himself in the same situation, in order to secure his sympathetic reaction, should be emphasized. Remember that emotion results when the subject, confronted with a response deadlock during the conflict of impulses within himself, endeavors to determine a direction for reaction.

Good general rules for the presentation of a trick or a program of tricks follow: Gradually slow down your tempo as you approach the climax of your trick or act. During the last few moments of your final effect ritard the action more and more. Pause two or three seconds after each IMPORTANT phrase. Pause almost twice as long just before the phrase establishing a point. These are general rules for insuring clarity and adding punch through captured attention.

Each trick may be regarded as a sub-climax. The first trick is started at normal tempo and that tempo is maintained except for a slight ritard at the end. On the next trick pick up the tempo again, but not quite so much as at the beginning of the first trick. Slow down a little more this time at the climax. The third number is picked up in tempo again, but not quite as fast as the second effect, and it is ritarded again during the last few moments. And so on with any additional numbers, each started not quite as fast as the preceding trick and ritarded just a bit more towards the end.

It must be emphasized again. This is not an invariable rule. But it is generally useable for any ordinary routine of tricks where the performer is confident and poised.

Tricks of timing, tricks of pointing are available constantly in the performance of top-flight entertainers. Notice their pace, their pauses, the inflection and accent. Listen to the tone and character of the voice. And if it is a visible entertainment as well watch the posture, inclination, movement and other handling of the body. A few notes, taken now and then when you see or hear particularly effective illustrations will soon supply you with a notebook of practical applications.

CHAPTER TEN

Surprise is always an effective expedient in the show business as it always compels a new or renewed interest in the routine. Almost invariably it results in a response on the part of the spectators. Surprise stresses the unexpected. Surprise is accentuated by emphasizing the conventional normal expectation until the last moment.

Surprise was one of the basic results of the doll house presentation detailed previously. You will note in that routine that while the unexpected appearance of the second girl is a definite surprise, yet it is not an illogical development.

Most effective surprise is based on this idea of logical but unexpected development. Because surprise is so radically removed from the normal course of events, it must be pointed and timed very carefully. Almost invariably the momentary pause just before the denouement is mandatory in order to allow the spectator to collect his wits for the impact. Otherwise, he might miss the point altogether.

Surprise is the basis of most short short stories, a type which has become increasingly popular within the past few years.

Almost invariably surprise carries with it PUNCH.

Tricks incorporating surprise are those such as the vanishing cane to silk, the production of a cigar or pipe after repeated cigarette productions and like effects. The cane to silk trick would be a better surprise if something more in character with a cane could be substituted for the silk, just as the pipe or cigar is in character with the previous productions.

By keeping the surprise in character with that which has preceded it, unity is maintained. A connecting thread of unity is a valuable asset. No first-class success in any type of entertainment, whether it be in the form of a motion picture, a stage attraction, a novel, a short story or any other type of diversion, can be achieved without endowing the undertaking with some degree of unity, no matter how fragile the connecting thread may be.

Now what is this unity?

It is the maintaining of a single idea from beginning to end. It is the stressing of this idea to the subordination of any other suggestion, although minor ideas may intrude occasionally.

Cardini's act is an outstanding illustration of unity. The idea of a slightly typsy Englishman being plagued by his tricks dominates throughout his whole routine. Slyter's drunk act also maintains unity to a superlative degree. Like Cardini's routine it is based on befuddlement through liquor. But whereas Cardini's character is only slightly spiffed, Slyter's conception is plastered to the eyes.

One way unity may be achieved, then, is by keeping the whole routine in character. The character emphasis need not be on the performer's condition. It may also be on the character's type—such as Spaniard, Englishman, Mexican, Chinese or so on.

Other character conditions might be, in addition to a condition of being under the influence of liquor, a condition of stupidity, or uncertainty, or like Peter Godfrey's priceless character of a shy, apologetic and somewhat uncertain Cockney. There is a limitless field from which to select an entertaining character. Any of the innumerable character qualities people demonstrate may be combined to evolve an entirely original angle of approach.

At random I can think of many: The loud, raucous, quarrelsome drunk. The ill-prepared, worried and awkward amateur magician attempting his first performance. Or the pompous, bluff, bewhiskered "professor" of magic. A Latin character, friendly, affable but totally unable to master the intricacies of the language. Caryl Fleming liked to perform as a good-natured but thick-tongued Dutchman.

Take a combination of characteristics, add them to a definite type of person, flavor this with a bit of nationality. This will create character. The character and his qualities will bring definite strengths and weaknesses. These are the pegs upon which you should hang your presentation and lines. The nationality referred to need not be necessarily foreign. There are many types of Americans from various localities, south, west, north and east.

Another way of maintaining unity is a series of tricks with different objects but all with the same results. As an example:

Everything the performer picks up vanishes. Or he is constantly being bothered with things appearing in his hands. No sooner does he put one thing down than another appears, to his consternation. Or he might have a destructive complex. Everything in sight is broken or cut or otherwise destroyed, but eventually all is made whole again.

The mental act is a good demonstration of unity. All of the effects are of a mental nature. Another type of act might be based on a character who is invulnerable to the ordinary hazards. He can handle fire with his bare hands, eat safety razor blades, stick needles through his thumbs, plunge blades through his wrist or neck. Some years ago one prominent vaudeville performer featured an abnormal appetite. He ate flowers, his shirt front, cigarette butts, cigars, stole a piece of music from the orchestra and contentedly munched that. He built that up tremendously so that no matter what he reached for—the bass fiddle, a chair or even an enticing blonde—they expected him to begin chewing on it.

Unity may also be maintained by doing all of the tricks with the same materials, like Ade Duval with silks, or a routine entirely with ropes, or water, or milk, or golf balls, or eggs, or watches, or coins, or cigarettes. Or anything else under the sun.

Or unity may be achieved by transferring an object with which a trick is done into another object with which another trick is done, and so on throughout the routine. Or with related objects like needles, thread, thimbles, cloth, sewing hoops, etc. Or with cooking utensils. Or tin cans. Or pen and ink and paper and blotters. Listing all such possibilities is impossible.

If the same object is used for all tricks, do different effects with it. In this way a handkerchief taken from the pocket may be burned and restored, stretched, dyed, produced, vanished, multiplied, penetrated and so on.

If different objects are used, you might try doing the same trick with all, as in the previous illustrations of repeated vanishes or productions.

To achieve unity, somewhere, in some manner a connecting thread, whether based on similar objects, an idea, on character work, or the attitude of the performer, or on effects, must tie the whole act together from beginning to end, like a clothes line with the family wash hanging from it. In this case the clothes line would be the unifying idea. It holds the whole together.

I can't stress this idea of some type of unity too strongly. It is a fundamental, if you are to register an outstanding success. It is not true of a magic entertainment alone. Nor is it exclusively true of the entertainment field. Unity is essential to any type of creation from the building of a house to the laying out of a city. From the creation of a musical composition to the painting of a picture. From the assembly of a rude sled to the planning of an aeroplane.

Nothing becomes an **individual** entity, a separately identifiable entire thing in itself, unless it is bound together as a unit. With unity it becomes a specific something. Without unity you have a nondescript miscellany.

This unifying idea may be bird, beast or fish. It may be physical—tied together with color, or a common type of construction of the props, or a common material, or a common shape. It may be mental—connected with a common moral, or a common theme, or a common outcome, a common attitude, or a common condition. It may be character—tied with a character flavoring from the same bottle, whether it be nationality, dialect, behaviorism, ambition, prejudice, weakness or what not. It may be unified through sentiment, romance, comedy, futility, nostalgia or any of the many atmospheric and emotional conditions. The ways in which an act may be given unity are truly limitless.

The more ways in which this unity may be strengthened, the better. One method of unifying the act is good. Many ways, all consistently binding the whole together, is superlative.

Almost the same may be said of character. No chef would prepare a dish without seasoning. Character is the seasoning which makes your entertainment dish palatable. Everything has character, even though the character is weak and uninteresting. Your job is to develop a quality of character in your routine that makes it tasty to the spectator. Otherwise you will have a mere assembly of ingredients, tasteless, unsavory, unappetizing, lacking zest.

Throughout the entire routine this character must be maintained. Everything you do must be influenced and shaped by this character.

66

It might be a case of playing an actual character in a specific dialect—broad of subtle. Yet it need not be this. Character may also be achieved by a lusty, devil-may-care attack on everything you may essay. Or it might be like the Cardini, or Slyter, or Peter Godfrey attacks cited before. Yet Ballantine, the comedy magician, burlesquing the serious magician, horsing all over the stage in a mock-serious attempt to sell the audience on his tag line, "the world's greatest magician," yet flopping on practically everything he attempts, achieves character in a different way.

People are interested in people. People differ from one another by differences in character. This difference is of superlative interest to other people. It is a fascinating, intriguing, irresistible attraction, impossible to ignore.

Character shows up in mannerisms, dress, conduct, beliefs, attitudes, manner of talking, manner of walking, grooming, personal appearance, reaction under stress and in many other ways. Consider the pictures you instantly receive with the mere utterance of character-revealing words. Languid. Stumble. Fumble. Listless. Prissy. Sulky. Jovial. Robust. Melancholy. Hilarious. Cheerful. There are so many of these words that bring a picture.

Character is revealed best, of course, by an individual's reactions to impediments, obstacles, stresses, emotions and the like.

But character is also revealed by the things a person owns. By what they are, how they look, what kind of care they receive, the type of coloring, etc.

What a person says is particularly illuminating, and how he says it. Consider: "Says you!" "The mater will be displeased." "Really!" "You're the guy I'm lookin' for." "I hain't gonna quit." "Stick 'em up."

The tone and character of voice counts: He grumbled. She shrieked. He growled harshly. She mumbled. His voice rasped. She cooed archly. His words were deliberate, slow, menacing. Her voice had a lilt. There was laughter behind his words. He said dryly. . . .

Mannerisms: He kept brushing imaginary specks from his clothes. She fussed with her purse. He chewed his cigar. She tapped her foot impatiently. She idly scribbled as she talked.

Dress: A loose-draped suit, festooning from his frame. Her dress drooped. Shapeless shoes with untied strings. His ears supported a too-large hat. A necktie so tight one more pull would have caused his tongue to pop out. Soup-streaked vest. Unpressed dress suit of greenly doubtful vintage. He wore a loud-checked suit, across the squared-off vest of which draped a heavy gold chain. . . .

Conduct: He grabbed a handful of cigars. He carefully pinched a single penny from his purse. With a flourish he produced a thick roll of bills and licked his thumb. He expectorated loudly. She belched, then giggled. He kicked the puppy viciously. He stuck out his tongue and gave a lusty Bronx cheer. . . .

Manner of walking: He ambled. She minced. He stumbled awkwardly. She dragged her feet after her. Prancing like a colt. Shuffling gait. Tip-toeing. He pounded after her. She danced towards him. . . .

Reaction under stress: At his laugh, tears welled into her eyes. At the slap in his face, momentarily his eyes flared, then he flushed and drew back. He saw the body, shrugged, then said, "That's the first time I ever saw him with his mouth shut." . . .

Consider the numerous pictures of people that any of the above illustrations suggest. Of course, these are by no means complete lists of such suggestions. Millions of ways of showing character are available to the entertainer, if he puts his own mind and ingenuity to the task.

But character-revealing ideas must be IN KEEPING WITH THE CHARACTER YOU DESIRE TO PORTRAY, whether the character is simple or complex. This is an important matter that should be given careful consideration.

Mention has been made of another important fundamental in attractive entertainment. We called it "situation." By this I mean predicament. Any set of circumstances into which a character may find himself, either through some action of his own or because of an action taken by another, deliberately or accidentally, from which it will take action on the part of the character to extricate himself, is a predicament. We call it being "in a jam."

Situations of this character, taxing the powers of the character involved, are extremely interesting to others. And, depending upon the seriousness of the predicament, to the character himself, of course.

Obviously it appeals as does any other conflict. It is conflict, conflict between the character and a situation. And the outcome will be either a victory or defeat for the one involved. The seriousness of the situation governs the seriousness of the outcome.

Magicians are familiar with many situations. The pull that breaks during a performance. The piece of apparatus that refuses to work. The spectator who lies about the card he selected. The old lady who stands up and insists she saw you put the ball up your sleeve. These are all situations. All of them are of great interest to magicians. It has been proven time and time again at magicians' conventions when some hapless performance is suddenly enlivened in interest for the other magicians when they discover the performer to be really in a jam.

These situations are interesting to magicians because they are situations in which magicians have found themselves and could conceivably find themselves again. They represent disaster. The magician subconsciously places himself in the same predicament. His chief interest is to see how the performer will overcome the difficulty, if he can overcome it. Or what he will do, if the difficulty is too much for him.

This is the meat of situation. The only difference in entertaining the public is that the predicament should be one that the spectators could understand, could appreciate and in which they could conceivably find themselves. With that condition, the heightened interest is certain.

A surefire situation for a magician is to lead the spectators to think that something has gone wrong. Other situations are the little boy with his arms piled high with eggs. Or the bashful little boy being introduced to the giggling little girl. Or the man watching his cherished watch being smashed up, or a cake being mixed in his best hat. For years magicians have been utilizing situations of all kinds to heighten their performances.

Russell Swann makes excellent use of it in his performance when he has a hat brought from the checkroom, identifies it and then goes over to the owner's table to give him a better view, while he stirs up a batch of batter in it. During the mixing of the mess, he also contrives to throw flour all over the hapless spectator, keeping his temperature just below the boiling point by assuring him, "It'll brush right off." All of this much to the heightened delight of the spectators. The "flour" does brush right off, because it isn't flour. But none of the spectators believe that.

We used situation at the close of the opening of the second act in the International Magicians show. The scene was laid in a modiste shop and a lovely young lady comes in to buy a bathing suit. She is in a great rush, and must try it on immediately. The flustered pansy floorwalker tells her that all of the fitting rooms are occupied, but at the urging of the girl, he finally suggests that the other girls can pile hat boxes around her. She may undress behind that.

During the floorwalker's absence the girl gets behind the hat boxes, which have been piled up in front of her, and proceeds to disrobe, throwing her clothing over the top of the boxes—the shoes, the frock, the petticoat, the stockings, the brassiere and finally the panties.

Upon his return the floorwalker shows great interest in the bare-shouldered girl behind the boxes. He seems reluctant to hand her the suit, in spite of the more and more insistent demands on her part.

He leans over towards one of the girls and asks, "Are those boxes glued together?"

The girl replies, "Certainly not."

A light comes in the floorwalker's eyes and he yells, "That's all I want to know." And with that he hits the stacked-up boxes a lusty wallop. The nude girl screams. But as the boxes tumble down the girl is seen to have disappeared.

Parenthetically I might add: When we did this number at the Headliner's Show at the national S. A. M. convention in Chicago a great many of my rakish pals who are also camera enthusiasts took photographs of a perfectly empty space, which fact was ruefully admitted to me the next morning by several otherwise respectable members of that august body.

Do I need any other illustrations to prove how situation, properly handled, can take the puzzle curse from a magician's trick? The situation was so strong that nobody cared how the trick was worked. I venture to say that the great majority of spectators never even considered that angle of it.

Truly of all of the situations of potential strength there is one made to order for the magician. If there is anything that delights an audience more than catching a smart-alec magician in a jam, I'd like to know what it is. This is a suggestion that can be used, with profit, no more than once during a program. But it is surefire.

CHAPTER ELEVEN

Proper costuming and careful grooming should be accepted as essential without question. When you are appearing before an audience you should look your best, just as you should look your best in the presence of anyone with whom you want to make an impression.

You wouldn't even consider appearing in your office or at a party in clothes that are soiled. You wouldn't think of appearing in attire that is out of date. Few people need be told clothing must be clean and well pressed.

Yet an astonishing number of magic performances are given where the performer's costume is not pressed and where the dress or dinner suit he is wearing is out of date, or frayed at the edges.

A performer, unless he is a character impersonator or a comedian, should never appear in any costume other than the very latest in cut and style, with the best of tailoring. Most performers insist that the cut and styling be a bit extreme. This is because a performer appearing as an entertainer has some distance and perspective to contend with, and decorative details must be accentuated a bit in order to be seen.

If there is any doubt as to your costume, whether it is in style, whether it needs pressing or cleaning, there is no doubt. Discard the suit and get a new one, if style is the question. Have the suit cleaned or pressed or both, if that is doubtful. It is a very good rule always to act when the doubt appears.

Performers doing occasional shows or infrequent appearances should always have fresh linens and freshly cleaned and pressed clothing. Always. For performers appearing in several shows daily, FREQUENT pressings and frequent changes of linen is the rule.

Every time you appear you should be carefully made-up. Your hair should be well groomed. Your hands should be clean, and your fingernails should be well manicured. Shoes should be spotless.

What has been said here, of course, does not apply to a performer playing a character. Many times such discrepancies help to maintain the character. As a matter of fact, if your clothes are not impeccable and if you are not meticulously groomed, you yourself are established as a character in the eyes of all of those strangers watching you. Why shouldn't they think you are a character? They don't know you. They don't know that even if your collar is soiled now, you sometimes wear clean ones. They can't know that the suit was pressed once, if it isn't now. How can they possibly know these things? This may be the only time they will ever see you. It's almost certain to be if you aren't well groomed.

Your routine should be as well groomed as the clothes you wear. You should know every instant of every program you do where everything is—exactly, not approximately. You should know what comes next, where it is, exactly how it works, what you are going to do with it. AND WHAT YOU ARE GOING TO DO WITH IT AFTER YOU HAVE FINISHED.

You should know exactly everything you are going to say. You should know WHEN you are going to say it. You should know HOW you are going to say it, as to voice, accent, speed, pointing and timing. AND YOU SHOULD KNOW WHAT YOU ARE GOING TO BE DOING—AND BE ABLE TO DO IT—while you are saying it.

You should know where your hands are going to be and how they are going to be held. There should be no doubt as to where your feet are going to be, how you are going to stand and the position of your body.

Be at ease physically and mentally. If you aren't, you are in no condition to appear before an audience.

The material you are to use, how it works, every movement of the execution of NECESSARY sleights, every movement necessary to operate any trick you are to do, should be thoroughly and repeatedly rehearsed UNTIL YOU CAN DO IT SUBCONSCIOUSLY, both the lines you are to say and the trick itself. This material should be so well absorbed that it **presents no problem whatever** during your entertainment.

Your entire mind should be free for **selling yourself to the audience.** Completely.

Every step of the routine should be paced off and kept unchanged, once settled. It should always be done that way, every performance. In this way you avoid awkward positions, stumbling and ineffective footwork.

If you are to stand still at some time during the routine, STAND STILL. Stand with both feet on the ground, with your weight on your heels. Stand with your weight properly balanced, breathing easily. Don't walk on your toes. Don't bounce and jounce and jiggle and mince. Walk. Or stand. Remember that these, too, are character establishing eccentricities. Of course, if you are playing a character, walk like a character, stand like a character. But if you aren't playing a character, if you don't want to be considered one, DON'T ACT LIKE ONE—EVER.

Make-up is a difficult problem. Few performers can really see how they appear in make-up, particularly where they are to be seen under artificial illumination. Footlights, flood lights and spotlights change the color of the make-up. Distance blots out details, and to be seen these details should be strengthened.

Formerly grease make-up was most generally used, either on top of a light cold cream foundation or without. Many performers use liquid make-up. For the most part, however, I believe that the Factor Pancake is most generally used now.

But regardless of the type of make-up used, you positively cannot use the street make-up colors. Entertainers MUST use the theatrical type of make-up in theatre colors.

Expert advice on make-up is far best. If you are in Hollywood you can arrange with Factors to go to their studios and have experts analyze you and select a proper pallette for your use. They actually make you up, and after all has been worked out, they give you a written list of the proper materials in the proper colors and show you how to put it on.

The next best substitute is to consult with friends who can advise you. Get your advice from someone with good taste and preferably from one who has had some experience. Experiment with various styles and colors of make-up until one is found most satisfactory for you. Then make a note of it and always do it that way.

As in the case of make-up, advice on clothes is always best from experts. Go to the best stores in your vicinity and find out what type of clothing will look best on you. Find out how the clothes should be cut, styled and tailored. Investigate, too, the matter of shoes, shirts, vests, ties, collars and the like.

This advice has been given from the man viewpoint. Most women know these things instinctively. Good grooming and appearance is an essential stock-in-trade of all women at all times.

What to do with the hands? This problem has betrayed more beginners than probably any other single thing. Use the hands when necessary, with certainty and smoothness. Make every move count. Some coaches in the theatre field advise that the movements be made as if the hands and arms were in water. This eliminates jerkiness and contributes smooth, graceful movements.

If there are times when you are standing before an audience empty-handed, drop the hands to the sides. They should hang there loosely, easily, without stiffness. Then forget them. Consciousness of the hands almost always betrays itself.

Facial expression should be natural and not strained. Avoid mugging. Avoid exaggerated expressions of all kinds. When you smile, smile easily using both the eyes and the mouth. Look at your spectators. Don't set your teeth. Don't look grim. Don't purse your lips and indulge in eccentric mannerisms such as whistling silently to yourself. Don't close your eyes when you do a sleight. Don't shy from a pull. Don't frown or scowl. Never betray anger or impatience or short temper.

Every expression should convey the pleasant things. Smile frequently. Smile easily, not stiffly. Smile as you would smile at a friend—that is, if you have any friends and like anybody. Smile at some specific person in the audience. It helps.

Of course, I must say again, if you are playing a character, or if your material is such that other expressions are necessary, don't adhere to these general rules.

But again, I must remind you, facial expressions also establish character. If you don't want to appear to be a character, keep your facial expression natural and unexaggerated.

The voice certainly conveys character. Angry people shout and scream. Nervous people talk excitedly in strained, high-pitched voices. Calm people talk with ease, with leisurely pauses, in low, well modulated voices. Fools and imbeciles mumble unintelligibly. Hearty men bellow and rumble and roar. Timid people whisper shyly. Thinking people are deliberate.

If you aren't playing characters such as these, you shouldn't talk in pitch or tempo like these. The normal, ordinary person is not ill-at-ease. He is not frightened or nervous. He is not timid. And he is not an imbecile.

Then, don't mumble to yourself. Don't shout. Don't talk in a high-pitched strained voice. Don't whisper.

Pitch your voice low. It carries better. It's tone quality is much more pleasing. Articulate carefully, sounding every syllable. Then you'll be understood. Pause a bit between phrases, so that your thought may be followed. Remember. You might know your lines so well that you can say every syllable rapidly and clearly. But the spectator doesn't know these lines and he must hear them clearly and grasp your meaning to understand you.

Don't strain your voice. It isn't necessary if your articulation and tempo are correct. Rehearse your lines in a large theatre or hall for friends. Let them correct you when you are not heard or understood.

Know where you are going to put your accents. A good trick is to underline the words to be accented, on the original script. Always read them that way. Rehearse them that way. Ultimately accent and the word will be simultaneous.

The best solution for the problem of being at ease is to be at ease. A thorough knowledge of your lines. A clear understanding of what you are to do and when you are to do it. Complete confidence in your ability to do the tricks you have selected. All of these contribute to ease.

If you don't know your lines well. If there is any ambiguity in exactly what you are to do. You aren't ready to perform yet. Obviously, if you aren't absolutely certain that you can do any trick well, that trick should not be used in public.

Stage-fright is not a species of fright. There is nothing frightening about a thorough knowledge and familiarity with your material. Stage-fright is more of an anticipatory nervous stimulation which evidences itself in the form of increased pulse, more rapid breathing, and an exhilaration.

Stage-fright can do no harm. It is the same type of lift an athlete gets just before the whistle blows to start the game or race. It is simply excitement. Some people overcome this in time. Repeated appearances help. Yet there are others who never can get over that first stimulation as they are about to appear.

Don't let it worry you. IF YOU ARE COMPLETELY CONFIDENT THAT YOU CAN DO YOUR ACT.

A dozen slow, deep breaths just before you go on will help to calm you down. A number of slow stretching exercises, rising up on your toes, is also helpful. But never condition yourself to the stimulation of liquor. This is dynamite. Soon you find yourself unable to go on at all without the alcohol.

If you must have a drink, don't do your drinking so its effects are part of your act. Many a performer has regretted conditioning himself to a point where he has to have the liquor or he can't perform.

Don't use ANY type of artificial stimulation or narcotic in an attempt to overcome nervousness or that "gone" feeling just before going on for your turn. Thus conditioned, you can never overcome a belief in a need for it. Soon these "treatments" must be stronger and stronger. You can't work without them. Finally you are all shot to pieces. Then you are finished—for good. I've known a lot of performers who have gone through the experience to their everlasting regret.

Actually, there is really nothing to overcome. If you suffer from simple stage fright, it is just a sign that your nervous system is functioning normally. Forget it. As soon as you start your routine it will go away.

But if you are nervous because you aren't certain of yourself and your routine, you are not sufficiently rehearsed.

Perfect smoothness is necessary in any routine. In no other way will your act seem finished to your spectators. Smoothness, which is a word meaning that you have planned thoroughly and well, gives confidence both to the performer and to his audience.

In smoothness rests the reason for rehearsal.

CHAPTER TWELVE

How can you gain confidence? Only by knowing that you are "right" and ready. You can gain this knowledge through the fact that you have been over the act time after time—perfectly.

Rehearsal is repeated private performances in preparation for public performance.

In the beginning, it consists chiefly in planning. Work out all details—every one—connected with the finished presentation. Settle upon an idea. Determine the type of character you are going to play. Even if you work "straight" you are still playing a character. You.

Determine the ways in which you can unify it, tie it together. Then make a selection of tricks and settle upon their order. Be certain that all of the tricks you select are **within your technical ability**, easily within your ability. Discard all which will tax your skill in the slightest. Then make certain that the complete routine, from start to finish, will come within your time limit.

Be careful that your time limit isn't too long. This is regulated considerably by the type of act, the place where it is to be presented, the conditions of presentation and the type of audience. Make your act just a bit **shorter** than the length of time you are confident you can hold your audience's **highest** attention. This idea of doing just a bit too little, rather than a bit too much, is smart showmanship. If they haven't had enough they'll applaud for more. If they've had enough—or too much—they won't want more. ALWAYS LEAVE THEM WANTING MORE.

In a night club you will be restricted to five to seven minutes. But you might have to do two or three different turns a night. You can't do much more than three average tricks in this length of time. If the tricks are long, two might be your limit. Where you have a single trick, leading up to a smashing climax that takes time to establish, if it can be made superlatively interesting for that length of time, perhaps one trick will do. But remember a night club requires constant "lift" or movement and great speed. This is because the spectators are drinking, their attention is difficult to hold, and there are many other attractions and distractions.

Vaudeville will give you eight to twelve minutes at the most. The competition is terrific. Eliminate everything that doesn't help the act to build up. Eliminate everything that slows down the tempo. Don't stall and don't waste time.

Casual performances at clubs and smokers should not run more than fifteen to eighteen minutes. Occasionally, family type entertainments will allow you twenty minutes to a half hour. But you are taking a chance on this length of time. Few performers have the personality and the material to continue to lift and move for this length of time.

And don't kid yourself about this time. Four minutes means two hundred and forty seconds; not a tick longer. Don't prepare an act that runs nine minutes and tell the master of ceremonies or the booker that it runs four. They'll catch you the first time and hate you to pieces. Maybe you know what happens to a carefully routined act when a large hunk of it is chopped out of the middle, or off the end.

So you have your tricks selected to come within the desired time.

Now if the act is done to talk accompaniment, fit the lines or spoken material to the tricks. Or the tricks to the lines, whichever is better. And you'd better have to fit the tricks to the lines than vice versa. It makes a better act that way.

Some people can write their own material. Most people can't. Probably it is always best to have your material written for you by a professional. He sees the act from the audience standpoint and can view you in perspective. You can't. Also he probably has a large reference library available. Also, if he's a professional writer, he probably knows how to write acceptable material. All of them don't. See that you get the kind that does. Writing is like fiddle playing. If you've never played a fiddle, the chances are you can't play a fiddle. You won't know how. It's the same way with a writer. He probably knows how.

Having had the spoken material coordinated to the tricks, the next thing to do is to put them together. Try them out. Rearrange and rewrite until everything seems right.

Then go to a music arranger and have your music score written. Insist that you get what you want.—Of course, this assumes that you know what you want. And are competent to know what is right for you.

Now put the whole thing together crudely and see how it goes. A first-class director would be of immeasurable help here. In fact, he'd be a big help from the very beginning. A director can put more lift and movement and zing and sales appeal and showmanship into an act in twenty minutes, if he is competent, than you'd be able to assemble in a lifetime, alone. One of the reasons for this is that he sees you as the spectator sees you. Also he has specialized, experienced technical knowledge which you can't possibly possess.

So if you can afford it, have the director or producer in from the start. It will be money well spent. If you can't afford a director, call in friends who have had some experience in show business or amateur theatricals. Call in several friends, if you have them. But for heaven's sake don't call in one of those amateur "conjurers" whose chief experience has been obtained at the Ladies' Aid Society or the Eastern Star. In fact, don't call in any amateur magician. If you must call in a magician, call on a professional who has had LOTS of experience. But, really, magicians should be left out. They have repeatedly demonstrated themselves to be poor judges of good entertainment. You see, the trouble is magicians like magic for itself. But the average spectator doesn't. He likes music and rhythm and comedians and sex appeal and such, the moron! But he's the guy that hires you. And pays the bill. And if you want to work for him, you've got to have your act the way he wants it.

Remember. He doesn't know a gimmick from the mechanism for a Kellar levitation. He thinks a pass is something girls slap your face for, and a pull has something to do with the police department.

If your act is silent, with musical accompaniment, just leave out that part that has to do with talk. Otherwise every thing I've said goes. Except that what I have said about music goes DOUBLE. You'll have to be extremely discerning with this. There's a lot of weight on it.

So now you have the bare bones of the act together. Of course, a costume is important. Bring in someone competent to advise you on this.

The next step is to provide for every physical movement in the execution of the routine. Determine the location of all of the props you are going to use, where they will be before they are used and where they will be placed afterwards. When these details are finally settled ALWAYS locate them in the exact spot determined.

Don't overlook that the location of some of these props will be determined by the sort of movement necessary to secure or dispose of them. Your original plan may have to be altered somewhat because of this.

Now walk through the whole routine, including entrance and final bow and exit. Make certain that the props are properly disposed for the most efficient handling with the least physical strain.

Now try it for the first time with the talking material. Fit the talk to the tricks and the tricks to the talk so that both coordinate. If there are any dead spots or moments when the action doesn't seem to lift, cut them out. **Eliminate all unnecessary movements.**

Extreme economy of talk and movement is IMPERATIVE.

I think about here is the time to explain what I mean by "action" and "lift" and "movement." They all have a special meaning in the theatre.

An act is like a set of stairs, always going forward and always rising. Going forward towards its ultimate punch and rising higher and higher in interest to the audience. Never should the stairs rise a few steps then descend a distance. Once you have gained a level, you must never drop below it. Neither may an act ascend a distance, then proceed on that level for a time. EVERY STEP MUST BE FORWARD AND **UPWARD**, SIMULTANEOUSLY.

Every word, every movement, every endeavor in an act must carry the interest higher and must approach closer to the climax. You cannot digress. You cannot pause. You cannot stop for by-play. You want your act to be a knockout. All right. Every pug in the fight game knows how to go after that knockout once it is in sight. Wade in and slug. Keep slugging, harder and harder and harder until the knockout comes. Your knockout is in sight the minute you step onto the stage. The preliminary sparring was done off-stage. The pug that stops to engage in a bit of fancy footwork or clever calisthenics gets his teeth kicked in. So keep on slugging. And I mean SLUG. That's why you can't waste any time in piffling trifles or fancy mitt-maneuvering. Stick to the act and its objective. Stick to it everlastingly, every minute. Allow NOTHING to distract you or the audience.

"Action" and "lift" and "movement," all mean this business of climbing the stairs. They mean going forward and upward. Anything that doesn't do that, anything that doesn't carry the act higher and closer to the punch should be eliminated. Eliminated ruthlessly, no matter how much you love the trick, no matter how well you can do it. No matter how pretty the apparatus. Throw it out—permanently.

Now you have the props properly set. You have the talk and the accompaniment fit to the tricks. The act has become a unit. Go over it with a fine-tooth comb. Find every way you can add to it—by accent, by interpretation, by gesture, by facial expression, by tone of voice, by movement, by posture. Make notes of all of these.

When this is done, when you are satisfied that you have explored the act from beginning to end to get the most out of it, you are ready to begin drilling on it. All that has gone before. All of the damnable detail exerted in putting the act together is called "routining" it.

When the routine is finished, you are ready to make it a finished routine.

A finished routine is possible only through tireless, unending, monotonous, incessant rehearsal. This grinding rehearsal is necessary to make every detail of the act habitual with you.

The rehearsal must be complete with props, talk, music and every movement. Do not rehearse parts of the act. Every rehearsal should proceed from beginning to end. Do the act completely, clear through—again and again. Go through it entirely three or four times your first session.

Don't practice individual tricks. Practice the whole act as a unit. The trick should lose its individual identity now.

If changes seem advisable, make them, but do not be too

critical. The main thing is to get the act within yourself completely and in detail.

The second rehearsal should see you through the entire routine, without stops, three or four more times. Do this every day. Probably, going through the act three or four times daily, in two weeks you will have it. But after the first day or so, don't make any more changes. Go over it again and again, clear through, each time.

If you make a mistake, correct yourself the next time through. Make certain that you won't make the same mistake again. All mistakes must be eradicated in the earliest rehearsals. Finally, before you can be satisfied, before you can be ready for performance, you must go through the act repeatedly without mistakes or prompting—many times.

If you allow the mistakes to remain while you are rehearsing, instead of throwing them out completely AT ONCE, you will be drilling that mistake into your subconscious mind AS A PART OF THE FINISHED ACT. And you'll never get rid of it.

And when you can go through the act time after time without mistake. When you have done the act so much you are thoroughly sick of it. When you and the talk and the trick and the music ALWAYS arrive at the same place at the same time. Then you have a finished routine. Then, finally, YOU HAVE AN ACT.

You have nothing to fear now.

As you play the act, undoubtedly experience will teach you better ways of selling it. Undoubtedly you will find some material should be weeded out. Unquestionably you will find other material—music, talk, tricks, or business—which will make the act stronger.

Make the changes.

CHAPTER THIRTEEN

It is well known that people like physical action. This is one of the reasons why sporting events such as football games, ice hockey, ice shows and other types of amusements featuring physical exertion are heavily attended by the public. In the theatre field the dancers, acrobats, trapeze performers and other entertainers of this type, where physical action is paramount, fill this requirement.

This kind of appeal is difficult to incorporate with magic. Yet it has been done. Carl Randall, one of the better dancers, used to do magic while he was dancing. Perhaps he still does. The well-known hotel dance team, The Hartmans, also uses magic in some of its dance routines. Benny Tolmack, one of the original principals in the International Magicians, does a tap and acrobatic dance routine while producing fans of cards, cigarettes and the like. It always registered well, extremely well, with the show.

Later Eddie Burnette took Tolmack's place. He, too, did a tap routine, and he used repeated cigarette productions while doing it.

If you insist on doing productions, there is no reason why many other objects cannot be produced, besides cards and cigarettes—silks or flowers, or multi-colored balls. Action can be incorporated with any of them. Even certain types of apparatus may be used for the production.

Yet the field is not limited to productions. An act incorporating a series of repeated vanishes or transformations or transpositions is quite feasible.

Anything in the magic line, if sufficient intelligence is given to the job of adapting it, can be incorporated in some type of dance routine.

Violent physical exertion, of course, has been used in escape type tricks for years, particularly in connection with certain rope ties or the straight-jacket. Some performers use violent action with handcuffs and box escapes, as well.

Undoubtedly there is a much broader field for exploration here. Violent sensational action, if the performer has sufficient intelligence to keep from making a superior ass of himself, has considerable possibility. The way violent action was incorporated with our presentation of the substitution trunk trick in the show has been explained.

Group coordination, where a number of performers act in unison, has been adapted to magic also. This massed coordinated movement is extremely attractive as will be realized when it is remembered that this is the fundamental of all chorus work in musical shows. Such a group at the Radio City Music Hall has become known all over the work.

I think it was Manuel who staged several group numbers with the Follies girls in one of the Ziegfeld shows. If I remember correctly it was a routine wherein all of the girls simultaneously vanished bird cages.

One of the night club lines in Chicago makes a specialty of group numbers performing magic. I have seen them use large phantom tubes, cigarette to silk changes, the mutilated parasol and other stock tricks, all done simultaneously.

Of course, in the International Magicians show we made a specialty of group numbers but in somewhat a different way. In the opening, as I have mentioned before, the entire company went into the audience and performed the miser's dream. Later the principals did the paper tissues to hats, using the comedian for the tissues to panties as a laugh punch. Also, at the close of the first half, the entire company did an original adaptation of the water fountains, and at the finale, as has been mentioned before, a bewildering series of productions by all of the principals, working simultaneously, brought the show to a smash finish. That this group work is effective is shown in the review of the show written by one of the critics when he said, "when . . . (they) . . . put on a finale, as they did last night, the total trickery is stupendous."

The inspiration for a closing number such as this came to me years before when I was arranging a magic club show for public presentation. Since all of the members did some type of production, I thought it would make a novel and smashing climax.

The idea had to be abandoned then because we couldn't make arrangements for satisfactory rehearsals.

At that same time I toyed with the idea of a group misers' dream number as well. For the same reason, it had to wait until the International Magicians show came into being. And the idea of simultaneous group presentation by MAGICIANS, not untrained girls, came into being with that show, I am certain. Strangely enough, I hit upon the tissue-to-hats number because I liked the song and wanted to use it. Having the group idea in mind as a feature of the show, and the musical background, the issue of the hat number was almost automatic.

This does illustrate, however, the manner in which ideas are born and how they are developed. The water fountain number came entirely from a desire to use the trick. It was entirely written around the trick. So here are four numbers. Two of them developed from a desire to use a lot of members of a club, one of them came from the title of a song and the other grew from a trick.

Of course, it is realized quite well that this discussion of group coordination cannot possibly apply to a lone unassisted magician. But most magicians carry assistants. Even two people can perform simultaneously, just as a pair of dancers do.

As a matter of actual fact it might be well right here to bring up an important point in connection with these long-suffering assistants. In my opinion characterless flunkeys, bell-hops and assistants of both sexes should be OUT. This servant and master idea, once permissible, is no longer good taste. This is particularly true when so many of the magicians are so palpably NOT the masters.

Once more I repeat: People are interested in PEOPLE. They are most interested in PEOPLE than they are the things people do.

Why not let that boy or girl assistant also become an individual? Why not let that assistant assert his personality also? Two personalities are better than one.

In forming our big show that's one of the first things we eliminated. There were no assistants. Whenever the help of someone else was necessary in a performer's routine, other PRINCIPALS came on to assist, as principals, as the nice people they were, not as flunkeys. I think that is one of the reasons so much comment was received on the friendliness and breeding and pleasantness of the members of the company. That positively got across the footlights.

This idea of a serf serving the master mind is really corny. It is not convincing. It is mere ostentation which is out of keeping in this day and age.

Where do you see any other entertainers using servants?

So now, you magicians who have an assistant, here is an opportunity to add that group number. Here is another personality to interest the audience. Make the act one with TWO magicians, instead of an act with one magician and an automaton.

Hints have already been given on how some group numbers have been presented. But there are many others. I remember one time we considered a dual manipulative act for a contest one of the clubs was engaged in. Although we never used the idea, it went so far as to get in a couple of rehearsals.

We planned on building the act up with backhand card palming as the basis. One performer was to stand at one side of the stage with the other on the opposite. Magician No. 1 would produce a card then toss it invisibly to No. 2, who would catch it out of the air. A sort of an invisible game of catch. In rehearsal the idea convinced me it had possibilities. We didn't abandon it. One of the performers became ill and we couldn't finish it.

Now a similar idea can be used in a two-person magic act. They don't need to play catch necessarily. Something, perhaps a bouquet, can vanish from the hands of one and reappear in the hands of the other. One magician could start a trick and the other could finish it. There are many comedy possibilities, as well.

Group numbers, for the average magician, are more easily available than one would ordinarily suspect.

Bill Larsen suggested a possibility to me some years ago. Why not have two or more magicians doing the cut rope trick simultaneously, each move timed to the others. The rope is cut and fixed, even cut and fixed again, if you want. At the end of the restoration, the ends of the pieces of rope are brought together and all of the pieces joined in one long length. I spent some time on this idea with a view to using it in my own show, but suitable music was a difficulty that was not satisfactorily solved.

Precise attack is always evident in any first-class production. This means that each number starts without hesitation. The performer starts to work without any preliminary fumbling or faltering. He knows what he is going to do and exactly how to do it. He does whatever his routine calls for with greatest economy of movement, talk and detail. He comes to the point quickly, does what he desires with confidence and concludes it cleanly.

Smoothness is almost another word for precise attack. Precision comes with familiarity with your material, with utmost confidence in your ability, with exact knowledge of what you are to do and how to do it, and with the certain knowledge that when it is done your audience will like it.

Precision means: For heaven's sake, do it and get it over with.

The word "economy" came in there. It is a mighty factor in the show business.

Economy means freedom from extravagance or outlay, with a disposition to save or spare. Every act should proceed from start to finish by the shortest possible route. This shortest possible route will not permit digressions. It will not permit pauses in the movement of the act while you orate about a trip to India. It will not permit breaking up the continuity of your routine to ring in some trivial, disconnected thing.

The routine must be free from extravagance with time. It must be free from extravagance of movement or words. Your outlay of time, movement, words—and, yes, tricks—must be limited to the bare essentials necessary.

Cut every unnecessary thing out of the routine. Retain only the bare essentials to sell the idea. But be certain you are not cutting something necessary to properly sell the act.

Economy means just exactly enough—not too much, not too little. Not too much talk. Not too much movement. Not too many tricks. Not too much time. Also: Not too little talk. Not too little movement. Not too few tricks. Not too little time. It is a matter of instinct and judgment and theatre and audience sense. You can't measure it with a tape measure or a scales. It is a thing of the mind and of the senses.

There's a good example of economy in Cardini's entire routine, but one little thing he does illustrates it perfectly. How often have you seen performers doing the untying silk? They laboriously twist it up, blabber about it, horse around with it, yell and beat their chests and run around the stage and generally raise hell all over.

Consider Cardini. He quietly takes the silk from his pocket. He twists it quickly, with a few deft movements. It unties. Again: He twists it, ties it. It unties itself just a bit more slowly. He shudders and discards the silk.

Just because you pay ten or twenty dollars for a trick that doesn't mean that you should take five or ten times longer with it than a two-dollar trick. Many of these ten and twenty-dollar tricks do not belong in your routine at all. Many that you can use aren't worth more than a few seconds.

I have in mind a twenty-dollar cigarette rising apparatus. The inventor knocked himself out giving birth to a long drawn out routine for it. So, when they bought it, ninety percent of the amateurs followed his entire exhausting dragged out version. Done that way, the trick laid a large fragrant egg. But one smart professional used it as it should be used. He took the pack from his pocket, tore the corner off and stood it on his table. One cigarette rose. It rose without twenty dollars worth of talk, frenzy and rioting on the part of the performer. After it was up, the performer calmly took the cigarette and went on with his routine, forgetting the twenty-dollar investment still standing on the table. Forgetting that two cigarettes could have been made to rise. Forgetting that he could have vanished a lighted cigarette and had it rise out of the pack lighted. Forgetting that you could place the pack anywhere. Forgetting all of the piffling features claimed for it in the advertising matter. The pack had done its job as far as the requirements of his routine were concerned. It had delivered its twenty dollars' worth.

While I think of it, something should be said about featuring a trick just because it represents a large investment of money. Professionals won't do it, but many amateurs save the feature spot on their program for their most expensive trick. Many times these expensive tricks do not pack the wallop and have not the strength to be featured. **Never allow what a trick costs**

89

to establish its place on your program. Never insist upon using an expensive trick just because it is expensive.

The only criterion as to whether a trick should be used or not is its reception BY THE AUDIENCE. The only influencing factor as to the placement of a trick is its relative strength WITH THE AUDIENCE.

Brevity is as important as economy. All trick plots should be SHORT generally. All routines should be SHORT generally. If you can do a trick in thirty seconds, and get the most effect out of it in that time, don't use three or four minutes. I've spoken before about the necessity of short turns. You have little choice in this in most professional engagements. Your time will be limited.

But where compulsion does not exist, your own choice of time will probably prevail. Take a tip from the show business. There is a reason why these acts are limited in time. The reason is purely psychological, although a lot of smart showmen wouldn't know what psychological means. Years of experience and observation have proven that audiences become restive and impatient when too much time is taken by a performer.

An audience will only allow its interest to remain with a performer as long as he arouses a lively curiosity or sympathy. Long drawn out repetitions of the same thing, or boring harangues, or periods of time when the action does not lift, dulls this interest. So the show business has finally hit upon the most practical solution. So limit the time of each performer that he can't lose the audience's attention for long. If you have a lot of personalities and a great variety of appeals, all aimed at the cross section of the average audience, mathematically his interest is bound to be maintained, even if it is only by reason of the fact that a new personality is soon to appear.

You are flirting with disaster if you take one second longer for your routine than you would be allowed under top professional direction. Of course, I know that you are certain your magnetic personality is sufficiently strong to interest an audience for long periods of time. That's the way YOU think. That's the way everybody thinks. But it isn't the way an audience thinks.

You must not loose sight of the well-authenticated psychological fact that each individual is more interesting to himself than any other individual is. To him, and that includes you and me, the most interesting thing on earth is himself. But, unfortunately, that isn't the way it works out with other people. Those people are more interested in themselves, the dopes! Imagine! To them THEY are the chief interest.

Since you are paid to interest THEM, and not yourself, you must forego your own preferences and play to the preferences of the people out front.

Don't take your own opinion as to audience interest retention. Take the opinion of an honest advisor who can see you as the audience sees you. You can't possibly appraise yourself. In case of doubt, it is better to err on the side of under-estimating your personal magnetism.

So make all of your numbers SHORT. Do them in the most direct manner possible. This was emphasized when we discussed economy. It was also emphasized when we discussed lift and action and movement. Probably you are beginning to realize that I have been using different words to say the same thing for quit a while now.

All of these various words—economy, lift, movement, action, precise attack—are merely different facets of one inescapable, all-powerful truth that permeates the show business from start to finish: Make each of your numbers as SHORT AS POSSIBLE. Get your act over with AS SOON AS POSSIBLE.

Get to the point. Be brief. Keep interesting them. Quit before they've had enough.

CHAPTER FOURTEEN

When it is said that an act or a show is efficiently paced, what is meant is that there has been a nice discrimination of time. It means there are no waits. That the interest does not sag. That there are no dull moments. That proper timing is in evidence as to the periods allotted for the respective units. That the units themselves display discrimination in timing. It means that the act or show moves swiftly, without delays, from beginning to end.

We have made repeated references to punch.

It may be defined as the creation of a forceful, striking impression, meeting the full approval of the audience, in such a manner that there is involuntary, favorable reaction from the audience. This reaction is invariably shown in a quick storm of applause. But usually accompanying it is some other type of expression in keeping with the emotion aroused. This may be laughter, whistling, gasps, cries of approval, shouts—or, if the reverse is desired, even disapproval. Punch is an explosion of emotion, caused by the built-up circumstances of the entertainment. It is an explosion that responds to the climax in the manner intended by the entertainer.

Such punches are obtained through many things. It may be a surprise. It may come from a sudden twist in circumstances that meets with audience approval. It may be caused by admiration for superlative skill. Or as the result of a daring effort. Or it may be caused by a sudden, overwhelming comedy development. It may be a response through some appeal to emotion. Perhaps it comes as the result of a thrilling passage of music.

In order to get punch, it is necessary that the emotions of the spectators be built up to the exploding point. That is one reason why the routine must always build up to a definite climax to which you have pointed from the beginning. That is why unity and economy are necessary in the routine. You stick to the subject and do not allow anything to distract or delay the constant pressure towards the ultimate smash.

And how can one accomplish such a smash?

By building up to a superlative degree the qualities already enumerated in this work.

The Rockettes secure smash by coordinated effort and a sensational exhibition of skill. The coordinated effort is in violent action. The skill is shown in the precision and training which results in some thirty-six girls performing as a single unit in unbelievable uniformity of rhythmic movement. Notice how many appeals the Rockette smash stresses—beauty, color, grace, music, precision, rhythm, coordination, skill, sex appeal.

If you can combine those appeals, simultaneously, in that degree of intensity, you, too, will acquire punch.

The presentation of the Doll House illusion, as explained, brings punch. This is a combination of surprise and a sudden comedy twist. But underlying it also is the beauty of the girls, sex appeal, music.

It is often remarked among professional magicians that magic acts do not seem to get the punch, make the smash impressions that dancing, singing, comedy and other acts get. **Might it not be due to the fact that the magician does not build up to a climax containing as many appeals?**

According to present-day magic standards, what is the appeal the magician reaches at the conclusion of his turn? Bewilderment? Surprise? Skill? Comedy?

Aside from these few, and rarely are they together simultaneously at the conclusion of a magic act, practically none.

The strongest appeals are invariably to the instincts, not to the mind. When you appeal to the mind, thought is necessary and sometimes reflection. To convince the mind, argument is necessary. And sometimes an argument is lost.

But the responses caused by our instincts are subconscious. They are involuntary. These instincts must respond to the appeals to them because we are constructed that way. That is why rhythm, beauty, skill, sex appeal, coordinated effort, physical action, harmony, melody, comedy, movement, youth, personality, romance, sentiment, nostalgia, surprise, situation, character, conflict, music secure reactions almost automatically. The response comes almost before we think. It is a subconscious response, a reaction to an instinct to which we are attuned.

Therefore, the securing of punch rests upon building up to a **group** of instinct appeals to a superlative degree. Not to bewilderment. That requires thought. Not to puzzlement. That, too requires thought. But to surprise. To comedy. To skill. And couple this with as many of the other instinct appeals as possible. Put in music, coordinated effort, physical movement, rhythm, color, beauty, sex appeal and any of the others possible. Use as many of these as you can. Build them up to as strong a degree as possible.

We combined coordinated action, music, color, movement, rhythm, nostalgia and many other appeals in the finale to our big show. And it invariably brought forth the results of a smash.

You can do this deliberately. You can start the planning of your act or routine with the smash climax first and work backwards. Don't leave anything to chance. It isn't intelligent. Deliberately incorporate the ingredients to make punch at the climax. That's the way they all do.

There are several minor matters that warrant further discussion before we take up specific applications of showmanship. Among these is the acquirement of grace.

This is an ease of attitude, an ease of action and an ease of posture. An ease of attitude comes from ease of mind. It is the child of confident knowledge and a sense of well-being. Nothing contributes more to this than a thorough knowledge of your routine and adequate rehearsals. Know your act is good and know that the audience will like you. This will bring graceful attitude.

Graceful actions are those movements, in harmonious curves, which convey no suggestion of stress or strain. Graceful posture shows no stress or strain. Grace is a matter of confident muscular control, of deliberate, timed actions. Some coaches suggest that the performer imagine he is in water and make all movements slow and graceful as would be necessary in moving about in the liquid. Whether this trick will fit your temperament or not, you need not worry about graceful movements if your movements are made calmly, without violence or jerky motions, in smooth efficient curves. The trick is to be calm and confident.

Effortless skill is almost identical.

The well-rehearsed movement, which is within the physical

capabilities of the performer, made without worry or without signs of physical strain, is a smooth one. Many magicians make serious mistakes when they attempt manipulative moves **beyond their capabilities.** There is no need for this. Keep your sleight-of-hand within your capacities. Make it look easy. If you have a small hand, don't try to use two-inch billiard balls. Use a size you can handle with comfort and confidence.

If you have a move of some character which you wish to use, don't put it into the act until you can do it well, faultlessly, without visible effort. Practice it. If, after a period of time spent in practice, you still are unable to do it well, you would better forget it.

John Scarne, probably the possessor of the most skillful pair of hands in the world, once told me many magicians make the mistake of trying to do a sleight or a move in exactly the same way someone else does it. He pointed out that all hands are different. Then he went on to show me how some moves are possible in one man's hands, whereas because of physical differences they are impossible in another's. Perhaps a too faithful adherence to another man's method may be your trouble.

It is far more effective to do a sleight or a movement that is easy for you to do, one that requires no worry or physical strain on your part, one that you know you can do well, than it is to try to feature the most complicated sleight in the world, if it means possible failure, worry or difficulty. Spectators like to see exhibitions of skill. But they like them to seem easy for the performer.

Surefire material is that material that has been audience tested time and time again. Surefire methods are those which have been proven effective repeatedly over the years. Certain tricks such as the passe bottles, egg bag, linking rings, WITH THE PROPER PRESENTATION have been known for years as surefire magicians' material.

Whenever a director has any doubt as to the ultimate reception of an act or a production, he interpolates certain material he knows will be surefire. This helps to carry the show.

Spectacle is a good old standby of the showman. It is principally masses of people, movement, violent action, strong colors, loud music and excitement. It is an ingredient within the capacities of certain types of magic shows, and to a lesser extent may be employed even by lone performers. Of course, the lone performer cannot provide masses of people. But he can use movement, violent action, strong colors, loud music and excitement.

More than one act and more than one show have been saved by resorting to this expedient. I must confess we resorted to it in the finale of our big show. And it worked, most effectively.

Perhaps you can try it. But let me warn you, I don't think it is quite enough, alone, without incorporating some of the other appeals in other portions of your routine.

Contrast is a showman's way of adding emphasis. Just as white looks whiter when contrasted with black, so should the fast and slow be counterpoised. If you want to emphasize loudness, immediately precede it with something extremely soft. The silent number stands out better in contrast with a talking one.

Contrast brings variety, and diversity is a stimulant to interest and attention.

Use contrast intelligently.

CHAPTER FIFTEEN

Without any doubt, comedy is the one audience appeal which supplies the greatest possibility to the entertainer who uses magic as his material. It is one of the most popular types of entertainment and is always in great demand. Our most prominent entertainers, and the highest paid, whether from the stage, motion picture or variety, are almost invariably comedians.

Often a gift for comedy is combined with other talents, such as juggling, ventriloquism, musicianship, singing, etc.

Many times performers start out as one type of entertainer and through comedy talents entirely shift their field to comedy alone. Offhand the names of many come to mind. W. C. Fields was a juggler. Will Rogers was a rope spinner. Cantor, Jessel, Jolson were all singers. Jack Benny was a violinist, as was the lamented Ben Bernie. Fred Allen was also a juggler.

When a magician essays comedy it is best that he forget entirely that he is a magician. I do not mean that he should not perform tricks. I do mean, however, that he should subordinate his magic to his comedy, that his magic should be used only for what comedy may be elicited by it. Magic, wherein a person performs a trick the means of accomplishing the effect of which is stressed as a puzzle, or a problem, is a very serious business. There is little in a problem that lends itself to comedy.

Russell Swann is one magician who changed his viewpoint and became primarily a comedian. Fred Keating and Louis Zingone are others. Clarence Slyter is another example. All of them use magic. But all of them stress particularly the comedy side.

Yet comedy, itself, is a most serious business.

Since the magician who desires to entertain with comedy is primarily a comedian, and not a magician, his study of how to gain comedy effects and how to sell comedy should be made OF COMEDIANS, not magicians who do comedy magic. How to do comedy best must be learned from the top experts at comedy. These men are the Fred Allens, Jack Bennys and the like. They have made outstanding successes at selling comedy, far above

These are the best school-rooms of comedy, the performances any comedy magician, and THEY SHOULD BE YOUR MODELS. of the best comedians. Don't confine your study to radio comedians alone. After all, as a magician you must be seen. Therefore, the VISIBLE comedy of the stage and screen stars must be studied. Don't affix yourself to any one comedian, either.

Study the methods and the ways of getting laughs employed by AS MANY GOOD COMEDIANS AS YOU CAN.

What I have said before about individual talents and propensities, and how carefully you fit the type of comedy you eventually attempt to your own equipment will have considerable bearing upon your eventual success. If you aren't built for certain types of comedy, you can't do them successfully. So try to analyze what type of comedy will fit you best. Then go after it.

Comedy has many phases. It may excite laughter by a faithful adherence to nature and truth. It may consist in the representation of lively and amusing incidents, droll characters or anything ludicrous or comical.

Humor is a species of comedy that flows out of a person. It runs in a vein. It is not a striking flow of wit but more of a pleasing and equable flow. It may display itself in actions as well as words. But humor is deep, thoughtful, sustained and kindly. It has more of sympathy and tolerance.

On the other hand wit carries with it intellectual brilliancy, quickness of perception and a talent for expressing ideas in a sparkling manner. Wit signifies knowledge, particularly that faculty of mind by which knowledge or truth is perceived. It is that faculty, usually spontaneous, of discovering agreements or disagreements of different ideas. It is a natural gift that seizes with an eagle eye that which escapes the notice of the deep thinker. It elicits truths which are in vain sought for with severe effort. It may be a single brilliant thought. Invariably it displays itself only in the happy expression of a happy thought. It is ingenious, sudden, surprising, keen, brief and sometimes severe.

Just as there are two kinds of comedy sources, humor and wit, so are there two kinds of comedy expression. Comedy may be expressed either in the form of a jest or a joke.

The jest is done in order to please others. It tells a story directed at its object which may be a person, thing, state of affairs and the like. It is intended to make its object laughable or ridiculous. It is seldom harmless. Even the most serious target may be degraded by a jest. Characteristically, it treats a thing more lightly that it deserves through raillery, repartee or hoax.

A joke is launched to please one's self. It is a sort of a game in which sport is made of its subject. It is usually directed at the person or on the person, and its chief object is to excite good humor in others or to indulge it in one's self. It may dispell dejection. Frequently it is harmless. Like the jest, in treating a thing more lightly than it deserves, it is intended to contribute to the mirth of the company. It may be applied to objects in general, whether a person or a thing or a condition.

Comedy may be of several general types.

If it is laughable, which is one general type, it is caused by objects in general, whether personal or otherwise. It may excite simple merriment independently of all personal reference. It concerns that which arises from the reflection of what is to our own advantage or pleasure. It is usually caused by the nature of things themselves. Ordinarily, it is without any apparent allusion to any individual, even remotely, except the one whose senses or mind is gratified.

If the comedy, however, is ludicrous, it comes from reflecting upon what is to the disadvantage of another. However, it is less to the disadvantage of another than it is ridiculous. A thing or person may be ludicrous without implying moral demerit or deprecation of the moral character of the object. It arises from a cause independent of the subject. As an example: The pompous, dignified president of a bank would be ludicrous if a suspender, quite by accident, should be seen hanging below his coat tail. It is associated more or less to that which is personal, and it causes laughter because it is absurd, incongruous or preposterous.

When something is comical or droll it does not leave a painful impression. Rather it applies more to the impression it produces. As for example: Suppose a man were to get on a crowded bus with a paper sack full of potatoes. Suppose the sack were to break and the potatoes should fall to the floor and roll about the bus. This would be comical, IF IT DIDN'T HAPPEN TO YOU.

Ridicule is a type of comedy that has laughter blended more or less with contempt. Its reference is more or less personal, and is produced by a strong sense of the absurd or irrational IN ANOTHER. The ridiculous always arises from reflecting on what is to the disadvantage of another. It is produced more by things than by persons. Usually it refers to things of a trifling nature. Usually it shows itself in verbal expression. We ridicule a person's notions by writing or in conversation. We ridicule that which is maintained by a person. Usually it has simple laughter in it. But the ridiculous springs from positive moral causes. It reflects upon the person to which it attaches in a definite manner and produces positive disgrace. It implies deserved contempt, and excites derision because of extreme absurdity, foolishness or contemptibility.

The humorous type of comedy implies the existence of wit. It is facetious, jocular, jocose, droll, comic, farcical, funny, laughable, amusing, diverting or entertaining.

Satire is a form of comedy employed in personal or grave matters. It is a personal and censorious form of wit which openly points at its object and exposes a folly or vice.

Irony is disguised satire, saying less than it thinks. It takes aim in a covert manner and seems to praise when condemnation is really intended.

Caricature and burlesque are closely related. Both are overloaded with exaggeration. But caricature is an overstatement or overcoloring, in humorous imitation of a person or thing, which greatly exaggerates defects or peculiarities in order to make its object appear ludicrous.

Burlesque is an exaggerated assemblage of ideas extravagantly discordant. It is a trifling or ludicrous imitation of an action or occasion.

All of the above types of comedy may result in laughter, mirth, ridicule, merriment, glee, gayety or any of the other synonyms for the general term laughter.

True comedy excites laughter by unexaggerated adherence to nature and truth. But when it takes greater license than true comedy, when it is full of exaggeration and drollery, when it makes use of nonsense and practical jokes, when it does not hesitate to make use of any extravagance or improbability, it becomes farce.

Since all of these various forms of comedy, coming to us through two sources and expressed in two ways, produce what eventually becomes a form of laughter, it is certainly advisable to discover, if we can, what causes laughter. Now I am well aware that greater brains than I can lay claim to have probed this matter of what causes laughter. It seems to me that I recall such hallowed brows as those of Spencer, Darwin, Aristotle, Brisbane and others having been knitted deeply on this subject. And without conclusive result, too.

So, even though I venture into what is almost certain trouble, I do so with the knowledge that much greater men than I have wrestled with this adversary, and have failed.

First of all, I can save myself a great amount of trouble by eliminating some complications. I'm not interested in all types of laughs—hysteria, pleasure, happiness, emotional, reflex, relief or covering up embarrassment. I'm interested only in what there is in comedy that causes laughter.

If we can find out what ingredients of comedy cause laughter, we can consciously apply these principles in creating comedy of our own—and genuine comedy deliberately created. It is worth trying, even though the result to me may only be the elimination of some intended comedy I have witnessed to my intense distress.

People are inherently cruel, even the most civilized of us. That which we call comedy invariably develops in connection with somebody else or the things belonging to someone else. We NEVER laugh at ourselves or at the things we own, except when sufficient time has passed so that we may view ourselves or our possession in perspective, and in a way look upon it and ourselves AS SOMEONE ELSE.

WE FIND COMEDY IN THE DIFFICULTIES, SHORT-COMINGS AND INCONSISTENCIES OF OTHER PEOPLE, CREATURES AND THINGS.

So there is your field. The only significant thing I can see at this moment in connection with the above statement is that not an inconsiderable part of Jack Benny's success has been achieved because he has consistently adhered to a policy of planning his

101

show FROM THE SPECTATOR'S VIEWPOINT. He, himself, has been that "other people." Benny is consistently the object of the humor in his shows.

Many other comedians have used this audience viewpoint when they have made the "difficulties, shortcomings and inconsistencies" their own, so that the spectators could laugh at them. I can think of The Mad Russian in the Cantor show; Fields; Bergen, who bears the brunt of Charlie McCarthy's sallies; Cantor and a great host of other prominent comedians.

On the other hand Fred Allen's type of humor is more mental. The chief charm in his programs is Allen's ability at "ad libbing," which is merely a stage technical term for spontaneous wit.

Now it strikes me that a magician is in a peculiarly advantageous position to make himself the brunt of the comedy in his routine. There is no more helpless, hopeless or totally demoralized performer in the theatre than a magician whose tricks have gone awry. A singer can hit a sour note, but he can recover during the remainder of his song. A mistake is only a minor part of a dancer's routine, or an actor's, or a talking comedian's. But when a magician's tricks go wrong, where is he?

Also, there is nothing more delighting to an audience than to see a magician get into a jam. It comes from some sadistic phychological quirk which always enjoys seeing the "wise guy" in confusion. In the usual magic show, where the secret of the trick is the important thing, the magician by the very nature of things, regardless of how charming a personality he has, is always something of the "wise guy." The so-called secrecy of the methods of operation puts him in that position.

Ballantine, the comedy magician who has been referred to previously in this text, uses this principal of a magician in trouble excellently. He just can't seem to get away with any of his tricks. Therefore, the audience is laughing at the character he plays.

The dividing line between comedy and tragedy, as has been said so often by many authorities, is extremely fine. We laugh at the difficulty of the other fellow, PROVIDING HIS DIFFICULTY IS NOT LIKELY TO BRING SERIOUS CONSEQUENCES TO HIM. We laugh at the shortcomings of the other fellow, PROVIDING THEY ARE NOT LIKELY TO BE

SERIOUS HANDICAPS TO HIM. The same may be said of the inconsistencies.

In all cases it is comedy, IF IT IS NOT ACTUALLY SERIOUS TO THE OBJECT, no matter how the object may feel at the time. THAT IS, UNLESS THE OBJECT IS AN UNSYMPATHETIC CHARACTER WHO DESERVES WHAT HE GETS. And even this exception sometimes doesn't hold. The character of Shylock in The Merchant of Venice was originally intended as comedy, but the consummate interpretations of capable actors twisted the character to a tragic one.

Now let's see what specifically is the cause of these laughs by examining the nature of these "difficulties, shortcomings and inconsistencies."

1—Physical difficulties which may bring a sense of distress or inferiority. These difficulties may be a black-eye, a toothache, a sore foot, a restriction such as being tied or handcuffed, or drunk, or stuttering. These difficulties are so numerous a list is impossible. However, usually the difficulties cannot be too serious to the person afflicted or the comedy becomes tragedy. I might cite the frequent references to Fred Allen's homeliness in his programs, or W. C. Field's appetite for whiskey.

2—A mental difficulty, or difficulties, which bring a sense of distress or inferiority. Such difficulties, too, are numerous. But typical examples are weak will, absent-mindedness, vulgarity, uncouthness, superstition, laziness, stupidity, ignorance and the like. Jack Benny is constantly stressing an undeserved conceit, penuriousness and a weakness for glamorous women. Max Rosenbloom stresses illiteracy. Hugh Herbert is jittery.

3—Exaggeration of the importance, distinction, size of or any other quality of a person, place, thing, condition, happening, talent, quality and so on. This is a frequent source of comedy as when the comic tells of the size of the lion he strangled with his bare hands.

4—Inconsistency in the association of persons or things. For example: A character of the type of Max Rosenbloom might explain that he used to be a professor of Chinese literature at some university. Or a physically weak character might explain how he beat-up on some notorious hoodlum.

5—A voluntary or involuntary misunderstanding of the nature, character, behavior, interest or importance of something or someone. As an example: A weak-minded character holding a lighted bomb, thinking it to be a hand warmer. Or a character booting the bride's father when he thinks him to be a rival for the girl's hand. Magicians use this when the kids yell for them to "open the other door" in the Dice Box trick.

6—A mistake of some kind. This is used frequently in farce comedy when the comic opens what he thinks is an ordinary door and falls down the elevator shaft. Or when he mistakes a real bear for a man dressed up in a bearskin.

7—An insult of some character may result in comedy, when a person attempts to promulgate an insult, or to avenge or prevent one. Almost every week the insult formed one type of comedy during the perennial Benny-Allen feud over the air.

8—An imitation supplies comedy. One character may imitate another. Or an imitation ring may be given the girl instead of a real diamond. A person or a thing may be the imitation, and the comedy may result in doing or acquiring the imitation or avenging it.

9—Repetition of a person, statement, saying, condition or anything else. Fred Allen had one character who constantly used the expression, "That I can. That I can."

10—A burden, in the form of someone or something inflicted upon someone. The old vaudeville act, "The Piano Movers," used such a situation with the little comedian constantly staggering under the load of the piano while his big helper stood around and told him what to do.

11—Loss of control. The control lost may be of the temper, of one's actions, speech, something, an animal, another person, a machine or almost anything. In the old Keystone Cops pictures, the driver invariably lost control of the flivver in which the cops were riding. A magician could use this in connection with the rapping hand, or the talking skull, or the bell. Charles Waller devotes a section in "Up His Sleeve" to what he calls "Perverse Magic." This is simply loss of control of the objects with which he is working to the extent that the objects do what they please, regardless of the performer.

12—Failure. Here a plan, a hope, an expectation, a person, a skill or something else, upon which the person is relying, fails at the crucial moment. Many comedy situations have been built around a comic's bluff, which fails when called. Or a tire failure during a chase brings complications. Or the inventor of a pair of wings jumps off of a building. Or at the launching of a boat the vessel keeps on going down—to the bottom. Failure of a trick, even when not intended as comedy, invariably brings laughs. Here's a good clue for a magician. This is one of Ballantine's strong points.

13—An expose of a person or thing. This is a painful subject with magicians, so I shall pass it by gently except to observe that it has always gotten a laugh when I've seen it done apparently accidentally. But classic comedy situations abound with exposures of imposters from "Charlie's Aunt" to the wizard in "The Wizard of Oz." The smash laugh at the climax of the International Magicians' version of the doll house was an expose.— No, no, not of the trick! Of the gal's boy friend.

14—Ejection. This is evidenced usually in a struggle to avoid or in actually having someone evicted from almost anywhere. As, for example, when the irate father tosses the unwelcome suitor out of the house. The immortal Cherry Sisters' act specialized in this form of comedy with the "hook" constantly menacing them.—As, perhaps, it has menaced even you or me.

15—A revolt or a reversal. This is illustrated repeatedly in when the worm turns. Or when the long-suffering husband finally turns on his termangent wife, as in "The Taming of the Shrew." A magician could use this to advantage by sitting down in the audience while a member of the audience acts as the performer—a self working trick might solve the technical problem.

16—Trouble. Threatened misfortune or mishap is always a subject of comedy. This may be brought about by the loss of someone or something, a threat from someone or something, an assault, or a test, or any other dismaying difficulty. I've never known a magician to fail to laugh when he discovers that a fellow magician has broken the thread for his, (the other fellow's) rising card trick, particularly if the accident happens during the performance. This could be used by magicians in a different way if circumstances should be so arranged that it

105

would seem impossible for the performer to do his trick. An example is the assistant's theft of the shell bottle in one version of the passe bottle trick. Russ Swann uses it effectively in connection with his version of the Rising Snake trick, when the snake apparently refuses to go back down into the basket.

17—A struggle or an assault to escape or achieve an objective. Some magicians use this for a laugh when they offer the pack for the selection of a card and then slap the spectator's hand and yell, "Not that one." Olsen and Johnson used struggle in their version of the straight jacket escape.

18—Meekly humbling one's self, in an attempt to gain something. Like when Benny begs Rochester to do something for him.

19—Ridicule of a person, quality, possession to disarm, demoralize, discourage or defeat some unwonted happening. Like the shaking comic who seeks to avoid being drafted by making believe he is a weak, undesirable character.

20—Victimizing someone in an effort to gain something. An old burlesque classic is a con game involving the betting of money. There are many, many versions of this. The handkerchief vanish where the handkerchief is thrown over the head of the unsuspecting spectator is an excellent example in the magician's field.

21—Resemblance. Where persons or things, totally different, are shown to bear a similarity in certain aspects. This may be used to praise, exaggerate virtues, to make fun of or even defeat someone or something. As for example when the rustic swain, courting his corn-fed gal, tells her she reminds him of his pet mule. Or when a comic compares the bravery of the bully who menaces him to the bravery of a lion. Or when someone compares an inferior person to a very superior person and the like.

22—Something which seems absurd is actually the truth. An example is when an enemy is discovered to be a friend, where a blundering person succeeds in spite of himself, a person succeeds because he didn't know he could fail; anything which creates an opposite effect from what is expected. Many magic tricks are in this class fundamentally. What is to be done seems impossible, yet it is done.

23—Just reward. It may be any sort of failure, punishment, loss, or discomfort inflicted upon an unsympathetic character. As when the ornery old squire falls in the mud hole. Or the officious cop gets bopped in the eye with a custard pie. There are so many of these situations that a list is impossible.

24—The destruction of something treasured. Tricks in which watches and rings are smashed, bills are torn and burned and other similar effects instantly come to mind.

The above twenty-four factors are what I believe to be the basic comedy situations from which all laugh-provoking situations arise. They may be used singly or in combinations.

The way to use them is simply to try to inject as many of these complications into your lines and situations as possible. Deliberately try to find where some of those conditions may be naturally applied to your tricks or presentation. Variety of attack and imagination in the use of it is of extreme importance.

A few more words and I shall be finished with what I have to say on comedy in this work. Because lines are so important in magic presentation a few final suggestions might be of help.

Among the ways in which wit may be utilized are (1) Turning an adverse comment back on the speaker; (2) To seize, apparently or really, a meaning different from that intended: (3) A remark which may be interpreted two opposite ways; (4) To cause harmless discomfort intentionally; and (5) To point out a weakness in a person's armor.

There are many incongruities and inconsistencies which are of great value in comedy. Some of them are (1) A dignified person in an undignified situation; (2) Two opposing qualities such as big words from a dumb-looking person, a definite type of person in contrasting surroundings, a large person with a small umbrella, etc.; (3) Misuse of big words; (4) Betraying a weakness such as a noble person having a weakness for wine, women and song, or a religious person swearing, a brave man who is actually frightened, a timid woman who is courageous; (5) Simulating a feeling opposite to that which the person actually feels; (6) Loss of dignity; (7) Embarrassment; (8) Hitting a man under the guise of a friendly slap; (9) A mistake of words, identity, date or place; (10) Clumsiness; (11) Excessive capacity; (12) Excessive work—especially to accomplish a small objective; (13) Excessive punishment; (14) Mistake of another's intentions; (15) Being prevented from doing something, like two lovers wanting to kiss; and (16) Surprise.

Dialect is also a potent source of good comedy.

CHAPTER SIXTEEN

Successful presentation of your trick routine or act is in direct proportion to the interest you can create in your spectators. There are two phases of interest that must be impressed upon the entertainer—the **creation** of interest and the **retaining** of interest.

Interest begins with catching the spectator's attention. There are two kinds of attention which apply to entertainment. They are voluntary and involuntary.

Involuntary attention is that we cannot resist, that which we give because we are sensitive to certain stimuli. Any sudden, unexpected loud noise is a good example—the blast of a revolver, the scream of a police or fire siren. A sudden difference in light conditions also illustrates the point. This might be a sudden darkness or a bright flash of light. This attention is passive. It is the result of external influence.

Voluntary attention is active attention. It is given as an act of free choice. When we give attention thus we THINK actively. THAT WHICH CAUSES US TO PAY SUCH ATTENTION IS SOMETHING WHICH PROVOKES THOUGHT.

Thought provoked attention is INTEREST.

When something **forces** itself upon our involuntary attention it can only affect our sense organs ordinarily. But when we take interest our higher nervous centers are affected. "It starts into action our sympathetic imagination, our reflective foresight, and sometimes our self-control."

Thought is provoked by any situation when our instincts and habits fail to deliver us automatically.

The normal person's interest is captured usually by the things he has to deal with ordinarily in his everyday life. To an audience of bartenders there could be no point in going into a psychological discussion like this. There is no point of contact with his everyday experience. To an audience of magicians there would be no point in going into the details of the complex actions, reactions and mechanisms forming the foundation of these elemental psychological principles, important as they are.

In that form they do not coincide with the magicians' experience.

Yet, by using only that portion of psychology which applies **directly** to the everyday experience of the magician, I can hold your attention. You are interested because attention is important to you, because it is within your common everyday experience, because it is a problem to you. AND YOU THINK.

There is the very fibre of interest and attention.

Literally, it means not to plan your material so that it is over the heads of your audiences. To hold their interest you must keep somewhat within their world, although a slight overlap into a wider area is not objectionable.

The classic plaint of the comedian, "My stuff is over their heads," is not an indictment of the audience, BUT OF THE ENTERTAINER. It is not a legitimate excuse for a poor performer. It is the proof of a poor performer. The obligation is not with the audience to pay attention to the performer. It is the duty of the performer to catch and hold their interest. He cannot do this if his material is too subtle, or outside of the realm of their interests. This state of affairs is a confession of failure.

An automobile mechanic will be interested in a trick done with an inner tube, a crescent wrench, an oil can or a piece of steel. He will be interested in a complication common to the problems he encounters in his normal life.

The normal woman will be interested in cloth, thread, silk, cooking utensils, canned food, vegetables and a long list of things and problems with which she comes in contact daily. The stenographer will be interested in objects and problems common to an office and her experiences in life.

A night club audience can understand and THINK ABOUT glasses, bottles, table cloths, dishes, liquors, cigarettes. An audience of children has the world of play and school. A men's club will be interested in playing cards, business deals, money, taxes, neckties, mens' handkerchiefs, cigars, cigarettes and so on.

The radio audience, the theatre audience and all other audiences, each peculiar to its sphere of daily activity, will have specialized interests, outlined by what they collectively encounter as a group in their daily experiences.

110

To gain their thoughtful attention, and I do NOT mean profound thought, their interests, your material and its delivery must be kept within the common field representative of the specific audience you are entertaining.

TO GET INTEREST YOU USE THINGS WITHIN THE COMMON EXPERIENCE OF YOUR SPECTATORS, SITUATIONS FAMILIAR TO THEM , PROBLEMS THEY ENCOUNTER, LANGUAGE AS THEY ARE ACCUSTOMED TO HEARING IT, BECAUSE IT IS THE ONLY WAY TO LINK THEIR THOUGHT TO THEIR ATTENTION.

Your audiences generally will come from three classes of people: (1) Immature and uncultured spectators; (2) Mature and uncultured spectators; and (3) Mature and cultured spectators.

The first class encompasses more than half the total population of this country—infants, children and young people too inexperienced to be interested in many things which appeal to grown-ups. But this class does not alone include young people. Many adults fall within it. It is claimed the average intelligence is that of a fourteen-year old.

To the second class belong our more prosperous people— the better educated farmers, skilled laborers, merchants, business men and, it is said, seventy-five percent of our doctors, lawyers and other professional men. These people have grown up and are accustomed to using their wits.

The third class is very small. These people are mentally more alert, more receptive and more analytical than most of us. Thus, as they grow older they accumulate an understanding of and an interest in a wide field.

It is obvious, of course, that the normal audience is largely of the first or second class.

So to gain interest you must gauge intelligently the class of audience you are to entertain. Bear in mind that while the second class furnishes your usual ADULT audience, the moment the members of an audience of this group become intoxicated they temporarily revert to the first. This explains why only the simplest and most direct tricks and methods of presentation will interest a group of people who are drinking, such as at certain types of smokers, night-clubs, and hotels.

111

It is for this reason that I feel that the average magician's apparatus, as such, is not scientifically correct to gain the greatest interest. There is nothing in the past experience of a truck driver, for example, that would cause him to become deeply interested in a red box with a Chinese dragon painted on it, unless what you are to do with it is within his immediate experience.

Do something with it DIRECTLY, like destroy it or restore it, and it is within his thought field. Cause it to float and it will hold his interest. But when you put something within it and then show it empty, he is not nearly as impressed simply because the interior construction is outside his scope of experience. It may puzzle him. He may wonder at the intricacies of its construction, but you will get a poor grade of attention.

The entire matter might be rectified by making that box look like something with which he is thoroughly familiar, such as a lunch box, the packing box for an inner tube, an ordinary packing box of wood or cardboard such as he handles.

This matter of thought experience evidences itself in many interesting ways. The needle trick is an example. The average spectator is thoroughly familiar with needles. He owns a mouth of his own. When you swallow needles the consequences are well known to even the most limited intelligences. He has tried to thread needles. He realizes how difficult it is. He knows it is impossible within the mouth and is curious as to whether you can do it and how you can do it. Does it hold his interest? It can't help it.

The presentation of the doll house as outlined previously is an example of pointing an unfamiliar object, the doll house, to the average audience's experience. A miniature house such as that is NOT common. But a home is. So is a romantic couple and their problems. By making the miniature house a model of the home this romantic couple is to occupy, the entire matter is projected within the spectator's thought-zone. The "other woman" is not an uncommon situation, either.

An emotion is an inner disturbance caused by the interference of several conflicting impulses to act. It is automatic. If you can set up a sympathetic emotion on the part of the spectator, and I do not mean sorrow or fear or any of the elementary

112

reactions, to a point where the spectator may begin to identify himself in the same situation, you are not only interesting him, you are making him a part of the act itself.

This explains why tricks like the needle trick, done under circumstances where you can CONVINCE the spectator, always sell heavily. It explains why that doll house routine met with such favorable reaction.

There are psychological reasons why the interest of a spectator may be retained only so long. He tires quickly. He tires more quickly when there is a single interest than where there are multiple stimuli. The usual magician's program concentrates upon one interest, puzzlement. If there are a variety of interests such as character, comedy, action, and others which have been discussed at length previously, you can hold his interest longer.

But, even with a variety of interests, this average spectator becomes fatigued.

This length of attention-holding time is a relative matter, too. If the acts which have preceded you have been fast and short, the spectator will begin to tire, having been conditioned to this type of brevity and speed, when you exceed the preceding acts materially in time.

If you want to discover what holds the attention and interest of the average audience, go to the best school in the world, the BEST acts. Pay particular attention to the topics stressed by the TOP acts. I mean, the headline acts in the theatre or on the radio or in the movies. They have reached the top, generally, because their attention and interest attraction has been SUPERLATIVE.

There is absolutely no advantage in patterning after a mediocre act. Mediocrity means nothing.

Pattern your own interest appeals upon the proven interest appeals in the better acts. That is surefire.

CHAPTER SEVENTEEN

The effectiveness of an entertainer varies with the types of audiences and with the suitability of his material to the specific audience he is entertaining. A given act, with certain material which has been aimed at a specific class of audience, will be most effective when performed for that audience. It will vary in effectiveness, with other classes of audience, directly as that act's interest appeals correspond with the experience of the cross section of that audience.

If an act, or any presentation from a single trick to a full show, can be planned so that it appeals strongly to all types of audiences, it will generally be more useful to performers who appear before various kinds of audiences. This is a point that should be obvious. The material in some acts is suitable only for a night-club audience. When this act is presented for a family audience, often it will be found to be downright offensive. Likewise, a routine that is patterned for a family audience wouldn't be acceptable usually in a night-club.

So it is necessary to give some consideration to the type of audience for which a routine may be planned.

Audiences divide about as follows:

(1)   A single individual, witnessing a pocket trick.

(2)   A small group of people, witnessing a program in a home, or at an informal gathering.

(3)   The family audience of mixed adults and children.

(4)   The mixed audience of adults only, comprised of people of average intelligence.

(5)   The mixed audience of adults only, comprised of people of exceptional intelligence.

(6)   The "drinking" audience of adults.

(7)   The audience of men at a smoker or banquet.

(8)   The audience of women only.

(9)   The audience of young people in their teens.

(10)   The audience of children from six to twelve.

(11)   The audience of extremely young children.

The character of the audience and the type of material most

likely to be effective may be judged by studying the possible characters and interests of the individuals making it up.

As an example the family audience is today the same type of audience that Herrman, Kellar, Thurston and numerous other magicians regularly played to in the past. It is made up of older men and women, settled adults and children of all ages. There is a simplicity that contributes to general mutual enjoyment. There is little artificiality about such a group. There is generally no competition, criticism or fault-finding among the individuals in a gathering of this kind.

On the other hand, the fourth group, the audience of mixed adults of average intelligence, is much different. Usually, as a group this audience is much more sophisticated, or at any rate fancy themselves to be. There is rivalry of dress and position among the women, and critical inspection and appraisal. The men, although not necessarily more intelligent than those in the family group, are usually professional or business men. Such audiences may be found in certain types of lodge entertainment.

Group five, the mixed adults of exceptional intelligence, is an especially good audience to a smart, capable performer, if he has the proper material. These people are educated because as individuals they are naturally investigative. The clothing, social position or financial standing which is important in the fourth group, gives way to intelligence standards. These audiences are usually found at literary societies, discussion clubs, forums, lecture courses and the like. The weak spot in this audience is the defense barrier they erect between themselves individually and other individuals in this group. This barrier reveals itself in a reserve in word and action which is difficult to break through.

The sixth group, the "drinking" audience, is a difficult one for the entertainer. Usually the audience is made up of scattered large and small groups. These groups are ordinarily more interested in themselves than in external influences like a floor show. Because they are drinking they do not concentrate. Often they are loud and boisterous and unruly. Occasionally the entertainer is confronted with individuals who are surly and antagonistic. It is difficult to gain and hold attention. Entertainment is secondary to food and drink and conversation. These people are usually not above average intelligence, with wits dulled because of liquor, to a point where little short of the most obvious will even interest.

The seventh group is similar to the sixth, except that since it consists of men only it is usually even more noisy and unruly, and it is frequently ribald. Drinking, this group is usually inclined to be rough. But sober, where the entertainment is connected with a lodge, it is a very amiable audience. Under this latter circumstance there is good-natured toleration of almost anything. The spirit is friendly. The object is simply one of relaxation.

The audience of women, the eighth group, is not at all common. Usually it is a women's club of some kind. Again you have competition and the distinctions arising from varying social planes. This audience may be considered almost unfriendly. It is critical of the performer, his appearance and grooming. Rarely will you find relaxation.

The young people in their teens make up the next division. There is competition between the boys and amongst the girls. There is inspection and critical appraisal. Reserve is a defense barrier difficult to break down. This group is particularly critical, alert, conceited—and yet willing to revert to the habits of childhood, if the change can be induced subtly. It is difficult to hold attention because of the awareness of individuals of the opposite sex.

The two children's groups are the trick performer's own field. Here you have spirited desire to trap the magician. There is a wholesome respect for the performer, a spirit of admiration, and yet underlying it all is deviltry and mischief making. Fundamentally, the difference between the two groups is that the older group will catch the magician if they can, whereas the younger children are simply interested. Both groups love tricks dearly. But the older group can become decidedly dangerous, if given the opportunity.

There are yet two more groups—still audiences, even though small. The first group is made up of a single individual, the person to whom you are showing a card or pocket trick. This person is friendly and the trick is performed, usually, as a bit of amusement for his benefit.

The same holds true of the second division, the friendly audience in a home or at an informal gathering.

This audience discussion is important because it lays the groundwork for an analysis of material suitable for the various audiences. Through an understanding of the essential differences in character of the audiences, it becomes much more easy to plan the material to gain the greatest effect. The underlying character of the group influences the state of mind of the individual spectator making up a unit of that audience. This state of mind changes as the spectator becomes a part of each different group. This, then, becomes the basis for material selection.

The magician's tricks and lines make up the material of his act.

The family audience is chiefly interested in relaxation. Profound mystery is acceptable in very light doses only. But even this is best cloaked in an interesting presentation. Comedy effects are chiefly desired. The pace is slow and leisurely. Elaborate magical apparatus is advisable. Always acceptable are the old favorites, the egg bag, the pudding in hat, the welsh rarebit, hat productions, the linking rings, rising cards, passe bottles, effects with live-stock, sleight-of-hand tricks of broad effect like the cards to the pocket or the multiplying billiard balls.

For the family audience the tricks least likely to meet with popular response are the spirit slates, mental effects and the usual type of card tricks. I believe it is a mistake to attempt such things as the X-Ray eyes, seeing with the finger-tips, muscle reading, the needle trick and the like.

The mixed audience of adults prefers a somewhat faster routine and a smarter approach. It is best not to perform effects subjecting a member of the audience to discomforture or embarrassment. The so-called "sucker" tricks are best left out. The properties and apparatus should be ordinary in appearance. Effects in which articles are produced from the mouth, like the needles and eggs from the mouth, are not in good taste unless performed with extreme discrimination and tact. The routines should be short with original angles of approach.

117

Mental effects are particularly effective with the educated audience. Effects like the X-Ray eye act, seeing with the finger-tips, contact mind reading and so on will receive considerable interest. Anything bordering upon the supernatural, like the rapping hand, the spirit slates or message reading, if properly "sold," will be sensational. Success rests almost exclusively upon refinement in the talking accompaniment and in profundity.

The "drinking" audience demands fast delivery, smart lines, smart appearance and broad effects. Many of the more successful performers work silent with musical accompaniment. Others adopt a fraternizing spirit and talk to individual members of the audience as to long-time acquaintances. The formula is hard work, fast work, loud talk, smart gags and direct simple effects.

An audience of men is interested in effects done with things in which men are interested——cigarettes, cigars, ropes, hand-kerchiefs, golf balls. Card tricks are popular if of broad effect. Avoid apparatus, trick tables, pretty drapes and such magicians' paraphernalia. Manipulative routines with cards, coins, balls and cigarettes interest them.

If this audience is sober you will have no difficulty in retaining interest. They like to see you make an individual spectator the goat. They like to have you take stuff from his clothing, break his watch, build a fire in his hat and in general clown around.

If drinking, this audience is like the mixed "drinking" audience.

Women are rarely interested in magic. Some of them resent it. Usually colorfully decorated properties will interest them most. The puzzle curse should be taken from the effects you do. The performer will receive very little audience cooperation. It is advisable to eliminate all effects requiring the use of spectator assistants. Use materials and properties with which women are familiar. Be careful to stay away from all types of vulgarity. Sympathetic silks, milk filtration, restored ribbons, spirit slates, message reading, diminishing cards, spiritualistic effects and that type of material are most effective.

Do not perform tricks where things are placed within the mouth. Women have a natural aversion to this type of performance. Use no card tricks except broad effects.

For the audience of young people in their teens, the repertoire should be similar generally to that for the mixed audience of adults.

Children are the greatest lovers of magic, as magic. But here you will find deftness and skill absolutely necessary. All of the "sucker" tricks will go here. There will be audible comments if the tricks are not done smoothly. Use livestock, hat tricks, productions, passe bottles, the egg bag and other old standard tricks. Don't try tricks based on misdirection. The misdirection will NOT work. Stay away from manipulative routines. Children are not particularly appreciative of performances of skill.

Keep in mind that the child's paramount interest is in discovering how the tricks are done. If you succeed in fooling him, you are a success. Do not perform tricks where something is destroyed or placed in the mouth. Fairy tale patter will go for the younger ones. The older ones will give you the razzberry, if you try it on them.

The performance of an individual small trick for a lone person is a comparatively simple matter, if the trick is of such a nature as to interest the particular person who forms the audience. A natural, friendly intimate approach is probably most effective. Nothing suggesting the theatre or theatre methods will be suitable for this type of presentation. This general advice holds true also of the small informal group. Everything should seem spontaneous and natural. **But, in spite of this appearance, everything should be carefully rehearsed and routined.** This is the most dangerous condition a magician can encounter.

All of the above is generalized observation. But it must be remembered that the groups remain individual, and identifiable as those groups, only so long as they remain in the environment of these groups. By this, I mean that the women's club group must be found in club surroundings. The children's group must be found where children would be normally entertained.

However, the moment these groups become part of a theatre audience, all theatre technique must be substituted for the more intimate techniques of the smaller groups.

119

Where I have made general references as to effects which may be found effective, that does not necessarily mean that the usual conventional presentation of those tricks must be used. On the contrary, to gain the maximum impression ALL of the appeals which are consistent with that particular type of audience, as detailed in this work again and again, must be employed.

I you intend to specialize in any of these groups exclusively, you should study the most effective entertainers in that group. Again I must caution you that I am not necessarily referring you to **magicians** alone. Rather I am referring you to the appeals employed by the foremost entertainers in these groups REGARD-LESS OF THE PARTICULAR METHOD OF ENTERTAINING THEY EMPLOY. It is WHAT they do and HOW they reach this group that is important.

The broader theatre expedients, as demonstrated by the top performers, acts and shows, still are fundamental. Yet these fundamentals may be varied and influenced by the specialized angles made necessary by the particularized characteristics of an individual type of audience. The theatre audience is a general audience and the general appeals will apply. The special group is a special audience and the general rules must be adapted to that group.

Yet there are no hard and fast rules that may be laid down for any one group. It is mostly a matter of presentation. Even effects and material which would at first thought seem to be unsuitable or out of place with a certain class of audience, properly presented from an angle that fits the group, can be made effective. Much of it is a matter of good judgment and audience sense. Experience with the various groups is the best guide.

While the words, "entertainment" and "amusement" generally have come to connote any type of pleasurable diversion, through popular useage, a study of the exact meanings of these will shed some light upon the type of material which might be found suitable in public performance for the average audience.

Amusement carries with it the common idea of pleasure. It kills time, especially leisure time. It keeps one interested or engrossed. It banishes reflection and lulls the faculties.

On the other hand, entertainment is more or less intellectual. It combines both the rational and social. It acts on the senses and awakens the understanding, and it reaches the most reflective people.

In Chapter Sixteen mention was made of the three general classes from which audiences come. Recalling that these distinctions are due essentially to varying degrees of maturity and culture, it may be seen that **amusement,** not entertainment, will reach by far the greater portion of average audiences. You should aim to **amuse,** because the first and second classes of people generally desire their pleasure to be of the type that does not require mental activity on their part. And these two classes are far greater in bulk than the class that prefers entertainment which is intellectual. The definitions of the three classes make this fact obvious.

CHAPTER EIGHTEEN

Under Chapter Twelve we discussed the fundamentals of routine to considerable length. Attention was called to the utter necessity of planning every minute detail specifically. It stressed particularly having a definitely planned location for every property, both before and after use. It stressed coordinating all actions, even walking onstage and exiting, to the music score. It emphasized the meticulous coordination of the movement with the spoken word. It insisted upon a COMPLETE interlocking of EVERY item—property, material, movement, talk, music, character.

So at this time we shall not again go over that. It might be well to once more turn to Chapter Twelve and read that again before proceeding, as the steps in routining several types of tricks will follow.

Any trick, to be properly weighed as entertainment material, must NOT be looked upon as a desirable piece of apparatus, as an interesting toy, as an intriguing puzzle or as a unit of anything. It is not. It must be looked upon much as a singer looks upon a piece of sheet music or as a violinist or pianist looks upon the written notations which are later to become music. In the written form, no piece of music· is actually music. It is merely a notation of something which becomes music ONLY WHEN IT IS PERFORMED. That is its real substance. Its existence becomes real only while it is being heard.

Now take a given piece of music. Let us say, for example, that it is "A Pretty Girl Is Like a Melody." You and I may look upon it as so many staffs, a collection of notes of varying time value and musical pitch, all a system of indicating symbols which when played as written will produce a melody identifiable with the given melody.

But an Andre Kostelanetz doesn't look at it that way. He realizes that the important consideration is how it SOUNDS. He is concerned with it only as MUSIC, not as paper with black marks upon it. So he proceeds to arrange it so as most effectively to present his interpretation. Tone quality and timbre of in-

122

struments are considered, they are brought into prominence individually at certain places. In other places they are but a part of the ensemble, sometimes many of them are not even playing. Moods are created by phasing, contrasts in tempo, contrasts in volume, emerging melodies, full rounded harmonies. There is no sameness anywhere in this arrangement. It is created to gain and hold interest, to convey an idea or a feeling. Played, it becomes the conductor's expression of his interpretation.

Performed, a trick becomes the entertainer's expression of his interpretation. The trick should not be looked upon as two metal cylinders, a couple of glasses and a pair of metal bottles which nest. It is not looked upon as a puzzle wherein a bottle and a glass, when covered with the cylinders, apparently change places.

On the contrary, it must be looked upon as the skeleton only OF AN IDEA. It is merely the notation, the melody, if you will, which you must EXPRESS according to your interpretation.

Routining is the making of this "arrangement." When the arrangement is performed, and only then, it becomes entertainment. Therein lies its only value.

Notice that every top entertainer, whether he be singer, dancer, instrumentalist, conductor, has a special exclusive arrangement, individual to himself, for every number he presents. This "arrangement" is his stock in trade. It carries his personality and his sales talk.

So it must be with your entertainment. That is why you must routine your material. It must be realized also that to benefit you individually the routine must be one tailored exclusively to your entertainment measure.

In the detailed routining steps to follow, please bear in mind that I am expressing MY individuality. It shows how I proceed to routine a number, to tailor it to my interpretation and personality, doubtful though the latter may be. This is the way I go about making my own "arrangements." It is extremely unlikely, since we are both distinct individuals, both of us would interpret any material identically. So these routining steps may be of value to you insomuch as they reveal mechanical steps. The mechanics of routining, as I do it, are revealed. But if you value your future reputation as an entertainer, you will set your sights to a higher entertainment goal than I have achieved in my intermittant attempts. To me personally my entertainment interests have been almost exclusively of secondary importance —extremely secondary—as compared to other interests in my dubious career. The achievements of **specialists** in entertainment, particularly not MAGICIANS, should furnish your inspiration.

All of which is a roundabout way of saying DON'T USE THESE ROUTINES YOURSELF. They're not made to fit you.

The presentation of a trick is actually the presentation of a small act, just as the performance of an act is in reality the performance of a small show.

All shows are planned after the three-act idea. Act 1 is the opening during which all factors are brought forward and pre-presented with a big gain in interest just before its close. Act 2 increases the interest and the complications. Act 3 brings all interests and complications to a climax which ends in a punch.

These three steps, even though smoothly blended together as a single unit, must be part of your routine.

Let me illustrate this with a pocket trick: There is a little trick on the market called The Ball and Tube. It consists of two small metal tubes which nest closely, and a metal ball. This ball is too large to slide within the inner tube, but small enough to slip within the outer one. Substantially it is a trick wherein the nested tubes are exhibited as a single one. The ball is demonstrated to be too large for this tube, yet at the performer's will it shrinks in size to the extent that it will slowly sink within and gradually reappear.

In considering the various trick plots possible, the one I chose was to exhibit the effect as a demonstration of hypnotism. The metal ball, highly polished as it is, would do quite well as a crystal.

The simple plot is this: Attention is called to the miniature crystal which normally rests upon the small metal pedestal. The entertainer explains how hypnotism works. The subject is told to fix his attention upon the highlight of the small ball, while the hypnotist passes his hand across the ball. As he passes the hand, the entertainer continues, he makes the suggestion that the ball is getting smaller and smaller until it seems to shrink in size sufficiently to fall within the tube.

During this talk, although the entertainer makes no reference to the fact that the ball has actually sunk into the tube, the ball does descend and rise to its former position.

"Now," says the entertainer, "that you understand the principle of hypnotism, let's see if it will actually work with you. Suppose you actually fix your attention on the ball. Suppose you allow yourself to dwell upon the suggestion that the ball is getting smaller." Meanwhile the entertainer is passing his hand repeatedly over the ball." Don't you really imagine that the ball begins to shrink?" The ball starts to sink.

"Isn't it reasonable to suppose that the ball is sinking into the tube?" The ball is quite deep now. "Or suppose I reverse the suggestion. Suppose I say the ball is beginning to enlarge." The ball starts upwards again. "Can't you almost imagine that the ball is returning to the top of the tube?" By this time the ball is back on top, and during the passing motions the outer shell has been stolen.

"Yet," says the performer plunging his free hand into his pocket and withdrawing a half-dollar, "this also is metal. You can bet real money like this that such a thing is impossible. That's why everyone knows there is no such thing as hypnotism." He puts the tube and ball in the spectator's hands, "Look at them yourself. You know it is impossible."

Thus, we start at the trick plot. With that in mind, we realize that there are certain secret things to do and certain matters to provide for. Since it is necessary to steal the outer tube and since the passing of the hand across the crystal is a reasonable gesture with a crystal, we decide to use this movement as the cover for stealing the tube. Because we have to seize the tube we alter the normal passing gesture so that the thumb and finger is on either side of the tube every time we make the pass. Since the tube must be taken off with an upward sweeping movement, we make the passing gesture an upward sweeping one. We do this because during the one pass when we actually steal the tube there will be no suspicious position different from the position repeatedly used. So the crucial move is well covered.

But there is still the matter of getting rid of the stolen tube. That's why we put in the business of the half-dollar. Since we use the right hand for the passing gesture, we put the half-

dollar in the right trousers pocket. This is a good final deposi-
tory for the discarded tube.

The routine, except for determining a position for holding
the tube and ball during the operation of the effect, is complete.
We work out the left hand position and we are ready to try the
whole trick as a routine.

A knowledge of the preliminary preparation necessary: In
this case, placing the half-dollar in the right pocket and nesting
the tubes with the ball on top.

**A knowledge of the coordination of the movements and talk-
ing lines:** These have been worked out.

**A knowledge of the weak parts to overcome and how they
will be overcome:** Here, the cramped position of the hand necessary in stealing the tube, the actual stealing of the tube and its
ultimate disposal. All overcome respectively by the final hand
position adopted, the repeated passing movements and the
plunging of the hand into the pocket under the guise of getting
the coin.

Plus a way of getting under the spectator's hide: Satisfying
his curiosity as to whether he is subject to a hypnotist's suggestion.

**All of these: Preparation, coordination, cover, spectator
interests, constitute routine.** All that is now necessary is thorough
rehearsal. Yes. Rehearsal of a simple pocket trick just as thoroughly as the rehearsal of a stage trick. If the trick is worth
performing at all, it is worthy of a finished presentation.

Now, honestly, don't you think this little trick plot and its
routine makes that effect more entertaining to the spectator?

Just as a piece of sheet music is not a finished performance,
so also is a bare trick not a finished entertainment item. It is
merely something to perform. It must be studied. It must be
practiced. It's possibilities must be explored. Then when you
begin to feel that you are familiar with it sufficiently to begin
interpreting it, go over it again. Examine every possibility.
Try to discover how you can make it effective from the spectator's viewpoint.

When you have properly routined it, have properly rehearsed
it, you may undertake to perform it. But not until you have
gone over it again and again in an attempt at perfection in every
phase. If you find some portion that you do not execute perfectly,

that does not coordinate smoothly, or if you find a place where your interpretation is not exactly as you would wish it, work on those parts until your misgivings disappear.

Even then it may not be perfect. But you have one tremendous satisfaction. You know it is the best you can do.

I believe good musicians are more painstaking in this regard than most magicians.

For the benefit of those who may still be doubtful of what routine means, I shall give you my definition: ROUTINE: A method of procedure, induced by circumstances, worked out with particularity, item by item, to be regularly followed until it becomes habitual, in the performance of entertainment.

The phase "induced by circumstances," is important.

Circumstances may require you to add a card to a deck. That must be provided for. You develop a good excuse for bringing the hand concealing the card to the deck. Of course, you know you do not put the card on the deck. You put the deck in the hand containing the card. The hand thus emptied must be emptied for a purpose ostensible to the spectator. It must be a plausible purpose. Perhaps that hand may move a chair, pick up a glass or gesture towards something.

But circumstances are extremely varied. These cover a wide field. They include the appearance of the objects used, where they are placed, what is necessary to be done with them. Circumstances also include what operations may be done in the open and those which must be concealed. Every detail of every trick, together with the personal characteristics and mannerisms of the individual entertainer, induces a new and different set of circumstances.

Routine the trick with the specific circumstances brought about by that particular trick, and you, in mind.

Note that "with particularity" is included in our definition. Every minute detail upon which successful performance is contingent must be provided for.

This does not only mean the moves. It means determining the **exact** place where each property will be prior to its use and the **exact** location it will occupy when the trick is done. It means consideration given to color harmonies throughout. It means the appearance of all properties—and your appearance, too. It means the words to use at any specific moment during the procedure. It means to predetermine which hands will be doing what and when.

There should be no fumbling or stalling. You can't do that because you know ahead of time exactly what you will do, when you will do it, what you will say, where your properties will be, where you will be and what the ensemble will look like.

One other part of the definition is important. Note that the routine should be **regularly** followed until it becomes **habitual**. If the operation of the mechanics of a trick becomes habitual, it may be done subconsciously. This means that your conscious mind can be devoted entirely to the SELLING of the trick during the performance. This is as it should be. SELLING the trick is more important than doing it.

I want to make this next example of routining one with a larger trick, in a style calculated to appeal to a family type of audience. The trick which Thayer lists as "The Haunted Temple of Quong Hi" is selected because it is familiar to most. To those of you who are familiar with Doc Nixon's version it is known as the Nixon Checker Cabinet. It is a variation of an old caddy trick explained in one of the Hoffmann books.

There is a slight difference between the cabinet I built for myself and the usual one. I used a roller blind, and my stack of hollow checkers is made up of individual checkers instead of the usual scored tube.

The mechanics of the trick follow: The cabinet has three doors in the front, side by side. Each door opens into a separate compartment. There is an auxiliary sliding section inside which corresponds in size to two compartments. If the sliding double compartment is positioned at the right, and if the stack of checkers is placed in what is apparently the center compartment of the cabinet, this stack may be moved to the left compartment merely by sliding the double section to the left, thereby leaving the center compartment empty.

Needed besides the cabinet is a stack of solid wooden checkers —I use eleven. And a duplicate stack similar in number and color to the first. Two duplicate glass jars of water are also necessary. The duplicate stack of checkers is hollow from the bottom up a distance sufficient to accommodate one of the jars.

Solid checkers are placed on top of the hollow section to make the stacks equal in height.

Each stack of checkers is placed on a wooden square to facilitate handling.

An ornamental cylinder, tightly fitting the hollow stack and covered at the top, completes the equipment.

In setting up the trick the sliding compartment is moved to the left. This brings the left section of the sliding portion behind the left front door. And the right section of the sliding portion comes back of the center door.

In the left section of the sliding portion is placed the hollow checker stack with the glass jar of water inside. In the right section of the sliding portion, behind the center door of the cabinet, is placed the solid stack of checkers. The black velvet blind is closed so that with all doors open only the solid stack shows through the center door.

The other jar of water and the cylindrical cover are placed on nearby tables.

Experiment with the apparatus showed that the best location for the cabinet was the center table. The jar of water was placed on the right stand and the cover on the left stand.

The lines are delivered in a simple conversational manner without any attempt at dramatics. It is a simple narrative of a good man and how evil is overcome by good—a surefire theme with a family audience, with a bit of sentiment thrown in. You will note that a bit of dramatic character work is incorporated in the dialogue. Notice the number of audience appeals that have been deliberately included. Also, the placing of the various properties adds physical action.

The directions, "right" and "left," are "stage right" and "stage left," respectively, as you face the audience.

The routine follows with the lines in quotation marks and the business and operating instructions in parentheses:

(Music: Theme song from "East Is West" background throughout.)

"I don't suppose any of you ever heard of Quong Hi. He was a wealthy Chinese philanthrophist who had built a magnificent treasure house to protect his wealth." (Performer walks to the cabinet and opens the door on the right as he says:) "The treasure house had three compartments. One was for Wang Foo, China's greatest warrior, who guarded the treasure night and day." (Opening the left door.) "Another was for Taio Li, China's most sagacious detective."

"The center apartment was for Quong Hi's treasure." (Opening the center door) . . . "Which consisted of eleven . . ." (Take out solid checkers and show them) . . . "distinct fortunes, each representing one month of the year in which Quong Hi spent doing good deeds for his fellow men." (As the checkers are squared-up and replaced in the cabinet:) "You will note that one month is missing. This represents the month during which Quong Hi retired from the world" . . . (Close all doors and release blind.) . . . "and spent his time in meditation and burning joss papers to the memory of his ancestors."

"Each morning it was customary for Wang Foo and Taio Li" . . . (Open right door and walk around to back and remove back of cabinet.) . . . "to open the back door and make a thorough search through the treasure house" . . . (Spectators can see through right compartment. Close right door, slide double section to right while talking and open center and left doors. Hollow stack is now visible in place of solid stack which is in compartment already shown empty.) . . . "Lest some interloper had concealed himself within during the night. The search completed" . . . (Replace back and close all doors, during which blind is pulled down again concealing two side openings.) . . . "the doors were once more closed. But whether closed or open" . . . (Open center door again.) . . . "you may be certain that Wang Foo and Taio Li were on guard."

"Naturally, eventually evil persons heard of this treasure and to get it enlisted the services of an evil old wizard who lived far out in the Gobi desert. This sorcerer caused a spell to be cast before the eyes of Wang Foo" . . . (Open right door.) . . . "and Taio Li" . . . (Open left door.) . . . "so that to them all life was temporarily suspended."

"Then the bandits broke open the door of the treasure house" . . . (Open center door.) . . . "and removed Quong Hi's wealth" . . . (Take out hollow stack of checkers.) . . . "taking it to a place they had prepared for it" . . . . (Carry hollow stack, on square block, to left stand and put it down, covering it with the cylindrical cover. Catch on hollow stack is engaged in slot of cover so that later when cover is removed stack will be carried away with it to reveal jar of water.)

"Now the most despised thing in all China was water because it was plentiful and therefore of little value." (Pick up jar of water from right stand.) "So as a gesture of defiance to Quong Hi and to show their contempt for Wang Foo and Taio Li" . . . (Place jar in center compartment.) . . . "they left the water in place of the treasure." (Close door at center and while fastening it slide double section to left, taking water from center section and bringing original solid stack back to center.)

Meanwhile Wang Foo and Taio Li slumbered peacefully. But Quong Hi's sleep was fitful and disturbed, and early the next morning he rushed to the apartment of Wang Foo.

(In a deep voice, imitating a Chinaman:) " 'Wang Foo! Wang Foo!' " (Knocking at the right door.) " 'Watched thou well during the night the treasure of Quong Hi?' " (Opening right door.) (In a different voice, also a Chinaman:) " 'Aye, sire. Watched I well. None so much as approached the door of the treasure chamber.' "

"Then Quong Hi rushed to Taio Li's apartment" . . . (Knocking on left door.) . . . " 'Taio Li! Taio Li! Watched thou well during the night the treasure of Quong Hi?' "

(In still a different voice: The left door is opened.) " 'Aye, sire. Watched I well. None so much as approached the door of the treasure chamber.' "

(Resuming former narrative voice:) "But at the crack of dawn the bandits hurried to the place where they had hidden Quong Hi's treasure. To their dismay" . . . (Lifting the cover and revealing the water.) . . . "they found the despised water. While Quong Hi's treasure" . . . (Opening the center door and revealing the stack of checkers. Background music begins to build up in a crescendo, louder and louder and slower and slower.) . . . "like bread cast upon water" . . . (Ritard tempo of speaking) . . . "had returned to him. Such is the story of Quong Hi." (Background music forte, bring up lights to full white. Performer bows slowly.)

Note the various audience appeals that have been incorporated within the routine—the background music, the various character voices, the theme, the conflict, the triumph of the kindly Chinaman, the change of pace and tempo, the music build-up and the added build-up of lights, all pointing to a definite triumphant climax.

Every maneuver in showing the conditions or operating the device has been provided for carefully under a natural excuse supplied by the course of events during the narration of the story. The attention is not on the performer but on the story. This story will get under their skins as my own experience has conclusively demonstrated to me. But it is intended only for family type audiences. Don't try it in a vaudeville theatre. It doesn't move fast enough. Also, it is too slow for a night-club.

The following illusion routine is one that I used successfully with the International Magicians, and later, altered to accommodate two persons, was received favorably in night-club and vaudeville performances.

The illusion used was the Thayer type guillotine, not the one with the falling blade, but the Chinese chopper version. This presentation was planned as a tongue-in-the-cheek burlesque of a typical sensational effect.

Instead of the usual red and gold decoration, it was believed that a combination of black and chromium would be more convincing, so the device was varied from the standard in this manner.

It was mounted on a three-foot high platform which was about twelve feet long and approximately four feet deep. At each end of the platform were steps. The platform, with the guillotine upon it, was located about "in three," which is about fifteen feet from the footlights. Behind the platform was a fulled silver backdrop.

The guillotine, with the blade inserted, was located in the center of the platform, but somewhat to the front. To the right of the right leg was placed a head of lettuce and a white towel. Behind the first wing, off stage right is a small pail, and on the opposite side is a large bucket. A ghost spot is placed in the footlights in such a manner as to throw a large ominous shadow of the guillotine upon the silver backdrop.

At the beginning of the routine the close-in curtains are closed in "one," hiding the guillotine from view.

132

All stage lights are out. As the performer enters from the right first entrance he is picked up by a white spotlight from the booth. With a perfectly straight face, and in a most serious manner, he walks onstage about five steps, stops and says in a low voice, "Removing the head from a human being is a very serious undertaking, as any of you will admit who have ever tried it." The curtains open behind him on a dark stage with the silhouette of the guillotine looming threateningly "Therefore, I'm going to ask you to be as quiet as possible while we attempt it once more tonight. . ."

The performer walks upstage and ascends the steps as the lights are brought full up white. "The device is known in China as a chopper." (Taking out the blade.) "It consists of two parts —a blade. . ." (Blade is leaned against the right side of the guillotine." . . . "and a sort of a wooden collar." (Taking off the upper half of the neck yoke.) "You will note that the upper half of the collar is removable. This removable feature is always necessary during the first part of the trick, although there have been times when we haven't needed it towards the end."

(Enter comic from stage right, who, listening attentively to the performer's explanation, becomes nervous and starts biting his finger nails. Girl and 2nd comic steps onstage down left.)

"In use," the performer continues, "A head . . . " (He picks up the head lettuce.) . . . "usually with a neck attached, is inserted within the opening of the collar." (Head placed in opening) "From then on, the operation is entirely automatic." (Performer picks up blade and inserts it in top of the channel.) "You simply insert the blade in the proper place . . . and push." (Blade is plunged through the lettuce which falls to the floor in two pieces. Comic spits fingernails (beans) into footlight.)

"But I might say, in China this device is not used for making salads." (Performer withdraws blade from guillotine.)

"We learn in all surgical operation that it is necessary for the tools to be kept clean and antiseptic, so with your permission. . ." (Still holding blade, performer picks up towel, blows his breath on both sides of the blade and polishes it with the towel. He also wipes off the neck of the guillotine and picks up any particles of lettuce which may have fallen on the platform.)

(He puts the blade back in a leaning position against the right

133

side of the guillotine.) "And now, what is to happen is this: The young lady's neck will be tightly encased with this collar, after which the razor-sharp blade will slowly descend. And then, if the lady arises intact, you will have witnessed a trick. If she doesn't, it will be something else."

(Girl starts tip-toeing off stage, but second comic grasps her and brings her to the platform, with some difficulty in view of her evident reluctance. The performer does not look at this by-play which takes place during the last two sentences.)

"I omitted to say that the young lady takes part in this demonstration of her own free will and accord."

(The girl kneels behind the guillotine and places her neck on the lower yoke. The performer tilts her chin up and gravely wipes her neck carefully with the towel, after which the second comic assists him in lowering the upper yoke and clamping all fast.)

As the performer lifts the blade to place it in the guillotine, the first comic dashes wildly off stage right and returns immediately with the small pail, which he places beneath the girl's head. But the second comic yells, "Wait a minute," and dashes off stage left, returning immediately with the much bigger bucket, which he places beneath the girl's head in place of the smaller pail.

The performer inserts the blade and starts to push. When the cutting edge of the blade is about at the level of her neck, he seems to meet with an obstruction and after a couple of attempts, stops and pulls the girl's head out a bit.

"Excuse me, please. There seems to be a vertebra there."

Slowly he pushes the blade downward, but he does it with his face averted away from the girl. Both comics hide their eyes. The girl screams. They all freeze, immobile, as if perhaps afraid the thing did not work. Looking away from the girl, the performer fumbles for the towel. He fumbles for the lower edge of the blade, head still averted, and wipes it with the towel. He brings the towel up within the range of his vision and finally dares to look. He sighs with relief and smirks with a pained expression. The others quickly look up.

The second comic, standing on the stage floor below the platform level, helps performer unhook the hasps. Performer lifts the upper yoke with right hand and helps girl to her feet with his left. Both bow.

The first comic stiffens and falls straight backward flat, in a complete pass-out. Blackout.

As in all routine examples, notice again that everything is completely provided for. A definite place has been established for all principal objects, and all auxiliary properties. Definite places and definite times have been established for all entrances. Bits of comedy and by-play have been provided for spicing and enlivening the proceedings. Definite plans have even been laid for which hand is to provide for each operation, and where everything is to go, in the last detail.

Where certain routine operations will take time and thus slow down the "lift," provision is made for assistance from the second comic in order to shorten the time.

And in order to add a final surprise punch, the pass-out of the first comic was provided at the very end—apparently after all is over.

Note how the minor bits of business add lift and take attention away from necessary preparations and operations which would otherwise cause a lull: The nervousness of the first comic. The fingernail episode. The cleaning of the blade and the "antiseptic" gag. The reluctance of the girl. The business of the pail. Even the bringing in of the second comic to speed up affairs. Of course, none of this is really a part of the trick itself, and has no place in the performance of the trick as a straight puzzle. All was added deliberately to increase entertainment value.

I chose this burlesque presentation as a travesty on the sensational tactics used by many magicians. These days sensationalism is downright "hammy" in smart company. It is my belief that modern audience do not fall for chiller-diller hokum any more. The magician who attempts anything like this straight and in serious character is courting a horse-laugh unless the audience is ninety percent moron. Magicians don't give the spectator credit for enough intelligence. They forget that in many audiences the average spectator is better educated, and often more intelligent, than the average magician.

Our show particularly was intended for the legitimate theatre audience, whose intelligence is much higher than the average motion picture or vaudeville audience. So we felt that a travesty on the conventional presentation would be recognized for the satire it was. The audience "got it." It was always received well.

CHAPTER NINETEEN

There are so many ways a performer may find a logical excuse for doing the trick he intends to do, or for using the particular thing he intends to use, that there is actually no excuse for dragging in some trick by the ears, willy-nilly. It doesn't make a bit of difference whether you intend to find a card, cause a handkerchief to vanish, find an egg in a black bag, cause a bottle to pass from one cylinder to another. Any effect you decide to do may be introduced logically, if sufficient time and attention is given to the matter when the act is planned.

There can always be a reasonable cause why you use a piece of string, a length of rope, a flag, a handkerchief, a box, a tube, a bottle or anything else. Having a reason makes for more unity in the routine. Admittedly finding a good plausible excuse is not always easy, but it can be done. Many times when confronted with a problem of this kind, if you don't try to force the reason, but instead file it away in your mind for a time—perhaps, over night or for two or three days—while you work out other matters, the answer will frequently come from your subconscious mind almost as an inspiration.

But it certainly is advisable to do everything in an act through some logical cause. I can't stress how utterly important unity is. It's the difference between a mediocre and a good routine. Insist on connecting everything up together.

Now after this excuse has been discovered, of course, this cause will color the entire routine. For example, if you find a good excuse for the Mora wands, your operation with them must again be connected up with the basic reason. Perhaps your act has to do with domestic difficulties. Suppose, for the moment, you are going to present your act from the viewpoint of a henpecked husband. Slant everything in the act from that angle, the lines, the props, the costume, the business.

Incidentally, instead of patterning your act after Cardini or Gali-Gali or Slyter, this is a good foundation for an act. Know why? Because it gets you on common ground with both husbands and wives in your audiences. Because it presents a human problem in which people are interested. Because it furnishes a suggestion for the most popular type of entertainment, character work. Because it has great comedy potentialities. And because it is away from the usual and the conventional. Several prominent character actors in the movies specialize in work of this type.

However, getting back to the Mora wands:

Again I must say I am using a common trick which is performed by many magicians. I do this because I want to show how as frankly a magical device as this, with a standard presentation as trite as they come, can be revitalized so that it can genuinely interest modern audiences in terms of their own experience.

First of all, because the wands are totally unlike anything within the ordinary spectator's experience, it would be difficult to find this common ground through them. But you can give the wands a purpose that is familiar. You can endow the wands with importance in connection with a familiar situation.

Did you ever pick up a strange-looking object in a hardware store only to discover ultimately it was a device for accomplishing some very ordinary, familiar, matter-of-fact household duty? The reasoning which led me to show these wands to the audience as something I purchased for the purpose of reminding my wife to put sandwiches in my lunch basket is devious and unimportant. But this is the way I use them:

"My wife never gives me enough to eat. I'm always hungry. When I go to work and open my lunch box, all I find is a piece of lettuce, an apple and two crackers."

"I like sandwiches, so one day I went to Sears & Roebuck's store to see if they had anything to remind my wife to put sandwiches in the lunch basket. . ." (Picking up the wands.) "The clerk showed me these. He said, 'They're nineteen cents each or two for thirty-five.' "

(Looking at them skeptically.) "I said, 'But how do they work?' He said, 'You put them in the kitchen drawer. Put a sticker on one that says CHICKEN SANDWICH, and another sticker on the other one that says ROAST BEEF SANDWICH.' " (Show stickers.) " 'When you want a chicken sandwich, pull the tassel on the one that says CHICKEN SANDWICH, and when your wife sees that tassel pulled out she'll know you want a chicken sandwich.' "

(With a delighted smile.) "I told him, 'I'll take two. I like chicken sandwiches and I like roast beef sandwiches.' So I took them home and showed them to the wife." (Working the wands with the ends together.) " 'See,' I said, 'If I want a roast beef sandwich, I pull the tassel out of the roast beef one. And if I want a chicken sandwich, I'll pull the tassel out of the chicken sandwich one.' "

"She didn't like it at all, as a matter of fact she said something about me wasting thirty-five cents for a contraption like that when she needed a new hat. But it worked very well for one week. One day I'd have roast beef sandwiches. Then two days I'd have chicken sandwiches. (Working wands.) Then another day I'd have roast beef sandwiches again. . ."

"But one day when I came home I found the chicken sandwich tassel pulled out and fourteen chicken sandwiches stacked on a plate beside where I keep my lunch basket. And the wife was in the front room reading Esquire. . ."

"I picked up the sandwich selectors and found she had cut the cord running down one and up the other. . ." (Show them separated.) "My wife's a mean woman. She just sat there reading Esquire with a nasty grin on her face."

"So for three weeks I ate chicken sandwiches. Finally, one day in desperation I yanked at the roast beef side . ." (Do so, and the other goes up.) "To my delight I didn't have to eat chicken sandwiches for a while. She had three dozen made when I did that. You get good stuff from Sears & Roebuck's. The man that invented that thing must have been married."

"So when I got tired of roast beef, I had chicken again. Then she took to hiding the selectors—one one place and the other another. (Still working wands.) But I'd always find them. And I'd have chicken or roast beef as I pleased."

"But you can't ever be safe around my wife. She started making them smaller and smaller. (Still working wands.) She made the chicken sandwich half as big as the roast beef sandwich. And when I went back to roast beef, that was half as big as the cut-down chicken sandwich. (Still working wands.)"

139

"But I fooled her. I hung on to the chicken tassel and I pulled as hard as I could on the roast beef tassel. (Do so. Both tassels are out now.) (Triumphantly.) Now the old battle axe had to give me TWO sandwiches. She couldn't starve me. . ."

(Sadly.) "I told you you can't ever trust my wife. She split the loaves of bread the long way and made me two sandwiches all right. Each sandwich was as big as a loaf of bread. I never got so sick of anything in my whole life."

"For three months I stuffed myself with those damn loaf-size sandwiches. Finally, I took the selectors back to Sears & Roebuck. 'Look,' I said to the clerk, 'You got to take these things back. They're killing me.' "

" 'What's the matter?' said the clerk."

" 'There's no way to shut the damn thing off,' I told him. 'Sandwiches, sandwiches, sandwiches! That's all I ever see. I dream about 'em.' "

" 'Do you mean you don't wish sandwiches, and don't know how to use the selector to show that?' "

" 'That's exactly what I mean,' " I said.

"The clerk looked at me pityingly. He said, 'Why don't people read the directions carefully? It very clearly says if you don't wish sandwiches you don't pull any string.' " (He reaches in the vacant space between the tops of the wands and pulls—just as in the invisible hair gag—and both tassels come up simultaneously.)

" 'Do you wish your money back?' asked the clerk."

" 'No,' I said, grabbing the selectors back, 'I'll get my money's worth out of them.' So I went home and beat my wife to death with 'em."

"Now I'm buying box lunches. They have a piece of lettuce, an apple and two crackers in 'em."

For some years now I've used the magician-in-a-jam gag as a presentation for the cut and restored rope. It is the identical routine I used, in Spanish dialect, with the International Magicians show. It is a presentation that depends upon subtility of facial expression to accomplish its strongest effect upon an audience, but it seems to fit my style well.

I wear a Mexican costume and speak in a broken English dialect.

"One time I hear of a treeck where you take one piece of rope, tie heem in one loop. Then cut the rope to feex it." (Cutting and restoring as you talk.)

"So I went to Tijuana and in a treeck store I see a sign which says they sell a trick where you take one piece of rope, tie heem in one circle and cut heem and fix heem." (Suiting the action to the word.)

"So I went inside the store and I said to the man, 'Have you got thees treeck where you tie the rope in one circle and cut him and feex him?'" (Cutting, but not restoring.)

"The man he say, 'What you want? The cheap way for to feex the rope? Or the expensive way?'"

"I say, 'The cheap way.'"

"He says, 'For a cheap-skate like you. Thees ees the way for to feex the rope.'" (Tie cut ends together.)

"But I say to heem, 'Thees is not what I mean. What I mean is to form the rope in the loop and cut heem——" (A look of consternation comes over the performer's face and he fumbles with the ropes, finally pulling them apart and to his dismay, showing that there are four, not two, pieces. He groans to himself, looks both embarrassed and flustered. Then finally, apologetically:) "My friends, I am in one damn bad jam." (There is usually a laugh here as the performer looks at the ropes helplessly. At the laugh, the performer talks towards the direction from which the laugh came.) "How you like to be up here and make one beeg fool of yourself in front of eight thousand people?"

(A bit more aimless fumbling with the ropes, during which the new cuts are tied. Finally, holding the rope in a straight length with three knots:) "For tonight only, as a special feature, I only feex the rope from here to here." (Indicating from the center knot to the top.) "Tomorrow night I feex thees part."

(Resuming the story:) "So I say to the guy in the store, 'How much for to feex theese knot?' He says, 'One dollar.'" (Performer indicates top knot and fixes it.)

"I say to heem again, 'How much to know how to feex thees one?'" (Indicating third, or bottom, knot.) "He says, 'Five dollars.'" (Rope restored at the spot. Then performer gazes speculatively at the middle knot.)

141

"I say again, 'Suppose I am performing at (Localize) and I make one damn bad mistake. How much to know how to feex thees?'" (Indicating knot.) "He say, 'That weel cost you five hundred dollars.'" (Show restored and toss to audience.) "So when I get five hundred dollars I find out how that is done."

Notice that the above presentation has been adapted from the old repeating handkerchief story. But it has been shaped and slanted and spiced with character work and situation and climax to the extent that it becomes intensely interesting to the audience. This is particularly true, if the apparent accidental "lousing up" of the trick can be made convincing by the performer.

The rising cards is an old stand-by and is always good with an audience, if it can be adapted to modern conditions and to a modern viewpoint. Using the Albenice swinging houlette with ribbons held by the performer and one spectator or an assistant, I have performed this many places, in night clubs, entirely surrounded at smokers and casual dates and even in theatres. Certain mechanical changes have been made in the Albenice device so that five cards may be made to rise instead of the usual three.

I force the Eight of Clubs, the Five of Diamonds and a special card, The Thirteen of Spades, in that order. The houlette is arranged so that the cards will rise in this order: the Ace of Clubs, the Eight of Clubs, the Five of Diamonds back towards audience, the Five of Diamonds with face to audience and a duplicate Thirteen of Spades.

"I want to show you how the magician's lottery works. Instead of numbers we use cards." (Show cards and fan them.) "The cards are all different so you can tell who wins the lottery. Now I'd like somebody to take one of the chances."

(Going into audience and forcing Eight of Clubs on a spectator close to stage, so all may see.) "Well, you have your number. Would you mind letting us all see? I tell fortunes with cards and perhaps there is something you should know. The Eight of Clubs. That means you are about to take a short journey which will be profitable for you."

(Having Five of Diamonds selected by another spectator.)

"The Five of Diamonds. A woman. And she is surrounded with money. You rascal!"

(Force the Thirteen of Spades but apparently forget to look at it. Quickly back to stage. Showing houlette.) "This is a magician's version of a fish-bowl. You will note there is no red tape connected with it. (The ribbons are blue.) Now we'll put all of the numbers in the fish-bowl. (Ask nearest spectator to step up. Or have assistant enter without delay.)

(To first spectator:) "Now what was your card? (Apparently misunderstand.) "The Ace of Clubs? Let's see if he's got the lucky number. Come on Ace of Clubs." (As houlette swings the Ace of Clubs gradually rises.) (Holding it up.) "That's your card, sir. You hold one of the lucky numbers. I don't understand. That isn't your card? Why I thought you said the Ace of Clubs. I'm sorry. We'll put that one back then. Every number's a winning number in this lottery. (Houlette swinging again.) Your card is the Eight of Clubs? Come on Eight of Clubs." (It rises.)

"Now the next card, please. The Five of Diamonds. (The Five of Diamonds rises back out.) I'm sorry. I must apologize for this bashful card coming up with his back turned. You see, this is a new deck and I haven't got them all trained as yet. Suppose we make the little fellow do it all over again. That's the only way he'll learn. (Five of Diamonds replaced in pack.) Come on up right this time. (The Five of Diamonds rises face out.)

"Now the last card please? (When he says Thirteen of Spades, look at him as if he is kidding.) The Thirteen of Spades! Please, no kidding. What was your card really? (When he repeats it again.) The Thirteen of Spades? Why I didn't think there was such a card. But then my folks wouldn't let me play cards when I was young, so there's lots about cards I don't know, as I've discovered in poker games. Okay. The Thirteen of Spades. Come up. (Skeptically, as if you still think the spectator is kidding. When it comes up:) Well. It is the Thirteen of Spades. I must apologize. I thought you were trying to get me in trouble." (You are showing card. As you finish last line, quickly look at card again as if you still don't believe it. When you see it is the Thirteen, shrug your shoulders in bewilderment.)

Please bear in mind that all of the above routines are in MY style of performance. They should not be used as they are given here. But they do show how it is possible to add new interests and variety and entertainment for the audience.

The examples shown were particularly selected from the repeating type of trick to show how to eliminate monotony in effects wherein the operation is repeated over and over again. These are by no means all of the ways of varying monotony. There is no limit to the variety, as you will discover if you give those repeating tricks you do some intense study. Try to make your attack varied. Contrast one relief with another. Try to bring in some human interest. This makes it particularly intriguing to the spectator.

The performer who undertakes to execute a trick in the conventional manner, or as the dealer's instructions indicate, is placing himself squarely in the quick-sands of mediocrity. These dealer instructions ordinarily are merely intended to convey information on the mechanics of operation and the handling of the trick in question. They merely tell you how to operate the device or go through the maneuvers necessary to accomplish an effect without disclosing the secret to the public. Uusually, they are not concerned with the presentation of the trick as entertainment.

To be entertaining, all tricks have to be endowed with a personal spark of life. They must have some human quality tied to them—a bit of character, a problem, some vital reason for being.

Dante accomplishes this integration of human quality in his presentation of the old ropes and handkerchiefs trick. Quite obviously he plays the character of an old rake whose purpose at the moment is to do a trick, but the light in his eyes and the way he looks at his girl assistant as he does the trick makes it clear to the spectators that his mind is on something else entirely. His eagerness to do the trick with a minimum amount of personal exertion, as he sits comfortably and has his assistants move the required handkerchief or the needed rope end to him, builds up character and audience interest and intriguing comedy. This presentation is truly in the modern style that magicians generally must come to adopt, if they are to survive as modern entertainers.

One of the best presentations of a small trick I have ever seen is Maldo's presentation of the six card repeat trick. I think it is probably the best thing Maldo does. Many times I've seen him step out in front of a vaudeville theatre audience with this little trick alone and knock them stiff. But it isn't the trick that does it, even though it is admitted that trick is a good one. It is the human quality that Maldo gets into it. The trick actually becomes vital to the audience.

As I remember it, this is substantially the way Maldo presents it:

Attired as a Mexican and speaking in broken English, English which must be frequently corrected as his assistant, with some embarrassment, calls his attention to his mistakes in whispers, Maldo explains a happening that took place at the San Francisco exposition:

"One day I am on the gangway. . ." The girl whispers. "I mean the Gayway at the San Francisco Fair, I see a man doing a trick where he counts—one, two, three, four, five, six cards." Suiting the action to the word. "Then he throws away—one, two, three cards. But when he counts the cards again he has—one, two, three, four, five, six cards. . ."

"I say to him: 'How is this that you can count—one, two, three, four, five, six cards; and then throw away—one, two, three cards, but you always have—one, two, three, four, five, six cards left?'" (Performing the second throw away and count.)

"He said, 'For one dollar I show you.' So I said, 'Okay.' Then he said, 'You start with—one, two, three, four, five, six cards. Then you throw away—one, two, three cards. Then you say, 'Abracadabra,' and when you say 'abracadabra' you will have—one, two, three, four, five, six cards left.'" (Performing the third throw away and count.)

"But on the way home I think maybe this guy he cheat me.— You know those guys from San Francisco. So I try it myself. I get one, two, three, four, five, six cards, and I throw away— one, two, three cards. . ." (To audience) "If I start with six cards and I throw away three, how many cards should I have left?" (Usually someone will say, "Six.")

145

"No, no. If I start with six cards and I throw away three I should have—one, two, three left." (He counts the remaining cards as three.) "But when I say, 'ABRACADABRA' that is a different business. Then I have—one, two, three, four, five, six cards."

But please don't misunderstand that the lines only are routine. The lines are important because they form the entertainment foundation for the trick. They color and influence it.

Once the angle of approach is determined, this influences the entire routine as to operation of the trick, position, business, music and so on. All of these are planned so as not to detract from the entertainment slant, to be in keeping with it. This holds true of interpretation, pointing, timing, decoration, character and all other subsidiary, but important, routine details.

There still is one important branch of entertaining that hasn't been touched upon as yet in this work. That branch is the often extemporaneous program done by the performer at a party or a gathering of friends.

There should be no really extemporaneous performances of this kind. Being extemporaneous, they must be poorly prepared. ALL poorly prepared programs, regardless of where they are performed, hurt magic and magicians.

So the magician should be prepared with a carefully routined and rehearsed "extemporaneous" program. Have it ready at all times. Make it short and snappy. As for a more formal appearance, know where everything is, how to do the tricks, what to say and all else—just as if it were your regular act.

The best kind of a routine for this purpose is one with cards that can be picked up anywhere. Don't do a lot of identification tricks—they lose audience interest fast. Do broader effects like the cards to the pocket, the thirty card trick, the four aces, and the like. Three or four tricks are plenty. Then quit. Quit before you wear out your welcome. Quit while you interest them. Then you won't get the reputation of being a bore, as so many card enthusiasts do because of a lack of judgment as to when the audience has had enough. That's what counts. What the audience thinks.

Such a routine, but requiring preparation, follows. I have

outlined a routine requiring preparation because I want to go into detail as to how this may be provided for.

The program is made up of five tricks which are quite well known among magicians. It should run about nine minutes at the most.

The "Extemporaneous" Routine

1—The Brain Wave Deck

2—A spelling trick

3—You Do As I Do

4—Remote Control

5—Card to Wallet

The Brain Wave Deck may be procured at almost any magic dealer. The spelling trick is one where the card is selected and replaced upon one of the halves of the deck. The halves are shuffled together and while shuffling with the riffle the performer "flashes" the card which falls immediately above the selected one.

My Remote Control method is varied from the original somewhat. The wax is affixed to one of the cards in a regular deck and the joker of this deck is placed over it. This protects the deck and the card until ready.

You Do As I Do is familiar to almost all magicians.

The Card In Wallet I use is the one with the celluloid plates bound together with multiple rubber bands.

The Routine: Performer comments on the strong part coincidence plays in the work of a magician, putting two decks of cards on a nearby table as he does so, a blue and a red.

Picking up the blue deck, but leaving it within the case, he says, "As an example, I'll show you. Suppose one of you thinks of a card. Think of three or four cards, if you wish. Whisper the names of those cards to a nearby friend and between the two of you decide on one as the one you want.—You have one in mind?" He pulls the flap out of the card case. "Will you please call it aloud so that all may witness this? The Nine of Clubs."

The performer takes the deck from the case and fans it. Very clearly it may be seen that all of the cards are back up except one, which when the deck is spread further open, proves to be the Nine of Clubs. "You see? Coincidence caused me to reverse

147

this card in the pack this evening long before I ever arrived here."

He places the blue deck in his pocket and picks up the red deck. "But coincidence goes further than that. Suppose one of you selects a card. I'll split the deck in half and put both halves on the table. Will you put your card on one of the halves?"

He picks up the deck. "Notice that I clearly shuffle the card somewhere towards the center of the pack and carefully square it up. Now while I was doing that you might think that I managed to get possession of it in some manner. So I'm going to fan the deck in front of you and go clear through it. Look at all of the cards. When I've gone clear through the deck, tell me whether you've seen your card somewhere near the center or not. But be careful not to tell me until I've gone clear through. Otherwise I might get some clue as to its approximate location."

He fans the cards, one by one in front of the spectator, and when he has gone through the deck he asks, "Did you see your card? Somewhere near the center I hope?"

He puts the deck down, saying, "I must insist that coincidence is strange and bewildering. For example, let us take a card at random—say, the Deuce of Diamonds. If I were to want that I should spell it out, taking off one card at a time. Like this."

He spells out the Deuce of Diamonds and on the last letter he turns over the corresponding card to show—the Deuce of Diamonds.

"But," he says quickly, "it is more complex than that. The deck is still here on the table. I sha'n't touch it. What was your card? The King of Hearts? Suppose you try it? The coincidence is not exclusively limited to me. Spell out King of Hearts, taking off one card for each letter, and at the last letter look at the card." The spectator does this and finds the selected card, the King of Diamonds, turning up on the last letter.

"I hope, by now, you are beginning to believe in coincidence." From his pocket he brings back the blue deck. "Just to prove it, I want one of you to take the red deck and I shall take the blue one. You shuffle my red deck for me and I shall shuffle your blue one for you." He places the blue deck in front of the spectator and pulls the red one over in front of him.

148

"Cut down into the blue deck and take out a card, just as I do with this red deck." He illustrates. "Now put your card on top of your deck, as I shall place mine. And carry the cut, burying the selected card." He illustrates.

"Now you give me your deck and I shall give you mine. You look through my deck and find your card and I shall look through your deck and find my card." When this is done, he places his card corner-wise in the spectator's deck and asks the spectator to do the same with his card.

"It would be a coincidence indeed, if the two cards should prove to be the same. Mathematically, it is possible only once out of one million eight hundred thousand times. But let us see—"

He turns over the spectator's card. "You selected the Five of Hearts." Pointing to his own card, "Will you turn mine over, please? Also, the Five of Hearts. I hope you are beginning to believe in coincidence."

"But it goes further than that." He takes a card from the blue deck which is now in his possession and without showing the face of it, lays it upon the table. "Will one of you put his initials on the back of this blue card?"

He picks up the blue card, still not showing its face, in one hand, and the red deck in the other. "I'm going to insert this blue card somewhere in the red deck, behind my back. I do this so that even I will not know where it is."

He inserts the card and brings the red deck out in the front again. He steps to a card table and quickly spreads the red deck face up. "I should like to have one of you pull one of these cards away from the others. Just slide it out, clear of the others. Now change your mind if you wish."

When a card is finally pulled out: "That is your own choice." He gathers up the remainder of the red deck, and still without showing the back of the selected card, puts this card face up on the face up red deck. He steps over to someone seated a short distance away. "You haven't been participating in this so far. Would you mind putting your initials on the face of this card?"

He cuts the deck, bringing the selected card to the center, and turns it so the backs are facing the audience. "Now I'm going to allow all the red cards to fall until we reach the one blue card in the deck. . ."

By twos and threes he allows the red-backed cards to filter from his hands onto the table-top, until he holds only the blue-backed card.

"Will you verify that the initials on this blue-backed card are those you placed on it?" After verification, he turns to the spectator who selected the card. "And your card was the Deuce of Clubs." He turns the card around and shows it. To the spectator who signed the face: "And these are your initials?" Then he smiles as he says, "It's simple, if you understand coincidence."

"I could do this all night, but one more illustration should be sufficient." He quickly scoops up the blue deck and mixed as it is, puts it in his pocket. "We'd better use the red deck for this unless someone wants to straighten out this blue one."

"For the last time I'm going to ask to have a card selected." Going to a spectator with deck fanned, "And I'm afraid you're the victim. Would you place your signature on the face of the card?" After it is signed: "And replace it in the deck. I'll shuffle it a bit just to complicate things." He hands deck to spectator.

From his pocket he brings a purse. "Now I'd like to have some honest person hold my billfold. That expression on your face might be kindness, or it might be honesty, I'm afraid I shall have to take a chance." He hands purse out.

He turns back to the man holding the deck. "Now you have the deck. Will you tell me what your card is?"

When the name of the card is called, performer says, "Isn't that strange? He couldn't have selected that card. By coincidence I thought of that myself, long before I came here. The feeling was so strong that I placed that card in my wallet. But look through the deck to make certain. It isn't there?"

To the person holding the wallet. "Will you please take the rubber bands from the wallet. If a moth flies out, don't let it alarm you. The moths have been bad this year."

The spectator removes from the wallet a pair of celluloid plates which are bound together tightly with multiple rubber bands. Between the plates is the selected card with the spectator's signature on it.

The performer remarks: "I think I understand coincidence quite well. But I simply do not understand how that signature got there. I'm so upset I'd really like to sit down and think it all over, if you don't mind."

Prior to the performance one of the cards in a regular blue deck is daubed with magicians' wax on its face. The Joker is pressed on the face of the card lightly. This double card is placed on the face of the deck, and the deck is inserted in its case. This pack is placed in the left coat pocket, lying on its edge.

The Brain Wave deck has blue backs to match. This is placed with a red deck, unprepared, which is also in its case.

The card in wallet effect is arranged for performance and secreted upon the person.

After the Brain Wave trick is finished, this deck is placed in the left coat pocket, beside the duplicate pack already there. It is placed on the side nearest the body, so no mistake will be made in bringing out the wrong pack.

As explained before, the selected card for the spelling trick is located by flashing the card which falls upon it in the riffle shuffle. When the cards are being shown to the spectator the identity of the card is discovered through the key. Beginning with this card, one card for each letter in the name of the card is pulled into the right hand, under the guise of showing cards to spectator. When last letter of selected card has been reached, flash the card next to it, the one to the left, and start spelling that card out. When you reach the last letter of the second card, break the deck above it—below it as you are looking at the cards —and carry this cut to what is now the face up top. Close up the pack. The first card spelled is this second card flashed— apparently a mere random selection by the performer.

In the You-do-as-I-do trick, the blue deck with the remote control card affixed to the back of the Joker is brought out. You shuffle this, as the spectator shuffles the red, being careful not to separate the prepared card from the Joker. Keep Joker somewhere near bottom of deck. When decks are exchanged and blue deck is in spectator's hands there is no further shuffling. Spectator, following performer's instructions, merely cuts the deck somewhere near the center and takes out a card. Performer goes through motions with red deck, as usual. When blue

151

deck somewhere near the center and takes out a card. Per-through usual locator card and proceeds in the usual manner.

At the end of the You-do-as-I-do, the blue deck is in per-former's hands, and prepared card for remote control is some-where near center of deck. This card is taken from behind Joker and brought out face down for the signature. Meanwhile, per-former picks up red deck and under guise of shuffling brings duplicate of prepared card to face of red deck. When prepared blue is placed in red deck behind performer's back, it is actually laid face-up on face of red deck.

Deck is spread face-up and red card pulled out. Red deck is closed up and card pulled out is laid face up on red face-up deck. This brings selected card on top of prepared blue when face is being signed. Cutting the deck brings the now double card to center. The rest is obvious.

At the end, put double remote control card with blues and gather them up. The wallet trick is done with the red deck which is still in order.

CHAPTER TWENTY

Heretofore, in our discussion of routine we have adhered to a general meaning of a particularized outline of detail for the performance of a single trick or effect. This, of course, means all of the detail that goes to make up the interpretation of a single number from a group that together will make up an entertainment unit.

There are many names for this group of units which constitute the program for a complete appearance. In vaudeville or night-club parlance this program is called an act or a turn. In unit shows or revues it is called an act or a routine. Where the program makes up the entire entertainment, such as a full evening performance it is called a show. And where it constitutes the full stage entertainment in a motion picture theatre it is called a unit.

For example: When the International Magicians was playing a full evening entertainment in a legitimate theatre, it was a show. When it was cut down to 45 to 60 minutes and played in a motion picture theatre, it was called a unit. The Pennies From Heaven number, our version of the miser's dream, was called a routine. Slyter's drunk act was an act or routine. John Mulholland's or Dr. Tarbell's lecture program entertainment is called a show.

Now we shall discuss putting together a number of these individually routined tricks, or entertainment units, into an act. I hesitate to call the individual numbers in a magician's program "tricks" because the word has come to connote the magical effect alone, without any reference to presentation. Perhaps it would be best here to refer to the units as **interpretations.**

With this in mind, then, we are to discuss the act, as a complete series of interpretations, making up an entire entertainment program. For our purpose, we are not going to limit the meaning to a short act. But we shall mean instead any program of interpretations of tricks, whether a short act of two or three numbers of a full evening's program.

In the beginning, however, our references shall be to the shorter routine as seen in vaudeville or night clubs or in casual club or smoker dates.

Ample reference has been made in this work before about limiting the time, about making it lift, about building it up with a series of sub-punches until it culminates in one great climactic punch.

It might be well, here, to add a few more facts on lift. "Lift" is accomplished when each number following another contains more and more audience appeals or stronger emphasis on the same appeals. Or the succeeding number may contain even less appeals, IF THE STRENGTH OF THE FEWER APPEALS COMBINED EXCEEDS THAT OF THE PRECEDING INTERPRETATION.

Lift means an arrangement of interpretations in such a manner that audience interest and entertainment INCREASES in intensity steadily. The audience attraction must always INTENSIFY. It must never waver. It must never recede. It is best if the audience attraction is never allowed to stay on the same plane. Entertainment value, as emphasized before, must **climb** the golden stairs.

These days acts are not mere collections of numbers. Acts are ideas. The stronger the idea—which means also the stronger the unity—the stronger the act. Stress of the human qualities and stress of the audience appeals plus personality make up this idea. It is relatively unimportant whether you do repeated card fans, pour cocktails from a shaker, or do the passe bottle trick, AS LONG AS WHAT YOU DO IS CONSISTENT WITH THIS ACT IDEA.

The cocktail trick, or rather under its original title Any Drink Called For, was done years ago by David Devant. And Chris Charlton was imported from England during the prohibition rebellion to do the same trick for swank parties in Florida. But Charles Hoffman made a specialty of variations of that trick alone and in a few years built it up from a first presentation at the P. C. A. M. convention at Hollywood in 1935, where it was a part of his magic routine, to his present act billing him as "The Highest Paid Bartender In the World." Joan Brandon, the blond magicienne of New York, also specializes in the cocktail trick with an elaborate set-up.

This idea of an act built around one trick has proven so important to Hoffman that press reports seem to convey an attempt on his part to restrict its use to himself. Of his success at this, there may be considerable doubt, as many professional performers, including Miss Brandon, have featured it for years.

Many performers, including Frakson and Cardini, have made a feature of manipulative acts including cigarette and card productions. If I recall correctly Hoffman also used cigarette productions in his original act of which the cocktail trick was merely a part.

Giovanni, and later others, has featured a single trick. His specialty is expert pocket-picking.

Many acts have been strictly sight acts, such as Cardini's act, or Slyter's drunk act, or the single act originally done by Lucille Hughes. In Cardini's case, of course, the tricks used were cigarette, card and ball productions. Slyter's act featured his character as a drunk, but included were his own multiplying whiskey glasses, production and multiplication of beer glasses, the standing cane, the color-changing scarf, alarm clock production and other effects. Miss Hughes featured showmanship of a very capable order with emphasis on her own delicate beauty. The tricks she used included the egg bag, the bouncing egg, the sympathetic silks and the vanish of a canary which reappeared within a nest composed of a grapefruit, an orange and an egg.

On the other hand, many magicians have featured comedy. Russell Swann makes a specialty of this type of entertainment, as does Ballantine whose act is very original.

John Scarne has featured demonstrations of fast gambling methods, and has been very successful with it.

However, this list does not exhaust the idea possibilities by any means.

Many angles from which to present a magic act may be found if a little thought is given to the subject. Charles Waller suggested a field that has been untouched as far as I know. This is a type of magic, referred to before in this work, which he called "Perverse Magic." In this type of presentation the tricks seem to take charge of affairs themselves, doing quite the reverse of what the performer wishes.

Another idea with comedy possibilities would be the performer adopting the character of a slightly worried and not at all confident magician. Suspense could be built up through character work, in a manner I am sure which would appeal to the average audience, which would give an air of uncertainty, not to say imminent disaster, to every trick he undertook to do. Somehow, in spite of the performer's awkwardness and palpable lack of training, the tricks would have a way of coming out successfully even when things looked most black.

Like the cut rope routine outlined previously, an entire act could be built up to a climax where it would look like the performer was facing complete disaster because of some very evident mistake. Yet all could come out well at the end.

Then, too, there is a wide field open to the character impersonator. Slyter's successful act is almost entirely due to his exceptional ability to play a part. Maldo, Pablo, Cantu and others, including Frakson, impersonate Spanish and Mexican types. Of course, for years there have been magicians impersonating Chinese from the time of the immortal Billy Robinson. But I believe the oriental character has been overworked.

A very good act could be devised for a character actor who could impersonate prominent people—movie actors, politicians, radio performers and the like. The act could be made up of a series of impressions of what kind of an act, for example, F. D. Roosevelt would give had he been a magician—or Marlene Dietrich, or Bob Hope, or Katherine Hepburn, or Edward Arnold, or Henry Fonda. It would have all of the attraction the usual impersonator's act would have, plus an entirely new slant.

To my own knowledge, not one magician has tapped the field revealed by Bob Hope or Jack Benny. Both of these chaps play the characters of quite ordinary fellows, not too smart, with the usual little ambitions and faults of the average person. Listen to either of these comedians and see what a peculiar slant their particular attacks would give a magician's act. I do not mean an impersonation of either of these men. I mean an act founded upon a performer acting and talking like these men, with similar weaknesses, vanities and other characteristics to those they exhibit.

There are so many sources for act ideas that it would be impossible to compile anything even faintly resembling a complete list.

An idea for an act may come from a particular type of character, as we have said before—Spanish, French, English, southerner, farmer, mechanic. Much comedy and good slants could be accomplished through coloring the talking accompaniment to dialects, or characteristics and mannerisms. There is also the impersonation field, as mentioned previously.

An idea may be created from an ultimate reaction you desire to impose upon your audience. Houdini did it with fear in many of his escapes. But there are so many other reactions possible— well being, happiness, laughter, nostalgia, sentiment, romance, beauty, and many, many others. You can start with this ultimate reaction and achieve a trick to secure it. Then work backwards from this climax to the beginning, selecting tricks or adapting effects to build up to this punch.

Situation is a good source of ideas. Put the character the entertainer is to play into a situation. This situation may be selected as the start of an act, or as its final climax. For example: the performer plays the part of a quite innocent book-keeper who has been mistaken for a notorious thug. Or a salesman suddenly confronted with a contract to sign and no pen to execute the agreement. Or a hapless motorist trying to convince a judge he wouldn't possibly break traffic laws. Most of the foregoing would be starting situations, although the salesman without the pen could be a climax.

Situation is a set of circumstances in which a character finds himself, a set of circumstances demanding that he do something. From this situation the act may develop to its climax. Or it may develop to a climax in which the character is in a better or worse situation.

Get the situation and work around it, selecting and adapting your program numbers to fit the circumstances.

It is said that the Chinese learned to make the products of the occidental world by carefully taking them apart. That's another way to create an act. Take apart a first flight act and

157

see what makes it tick. But be sure not to take a magic act apart. I've said before that your guidance should come from the very TOP of the theatre field and magicians are not at the top.

Take the act apart and see what makes it go. Was the act straight or in character? How long was it? What was the entertainer's attitude towards the audience? What quality in his work captured their attention at the start? Why did they like him? What steps were there in the act's progress to a climax? What was that climax? How was it achieved? How many numbers did the entertainer use? Time them individually. What did each accomplish?

You can ask yourself scores of questions like this about any big-time act. The questions should concern the character of the act, the dressing, time, nature of the punches, appeals to spectators, etc. Then use this as a blueprint for your own act. I don't mean to steal the man's act. That will provoke him no end. Use the skeleton framework of his act for your framework. Then hang your own material on it.

The material that makes up the act, this clothing on top of the framework, is what makes up the act's individuality to the audience. All acts are built on comparatively few basic formulas. These may be discovered by taking the acts apart. Then you can build your own act, from the magic theme, to this formula.

Has this been done before? Of course. That's where I got the formula for the International Magicians. I have always admired Clifford Fischer's formula for the Folies Bergere. Among stage directors it was known as possibly the fastest, most entertaining and most sweeping in the world. It happened that I was the technical director for the planning of the auditorium in which the Folies Bergere played at the San Francisco Exposition. Later I was in charge of the design and construction of the curtains for this stage.

So while I was there I made an intensive study of this formula for use with the International Magicians show, which was in mind even then. When the show was first produced it took some time to whip it into what I ultimately had in mind.

I don't know that I ever told anyone what my formula pattern came from, but listen to what Leon Simon said in the

Los Angeles Evening News after our opening there: "The most entertaining magic show ever presented on any stage. But it is more than hocus pocus that gives the show its high entertainment quality. Fitzkee . . . has endowed it with the smartness and lightning-like pace of a **Folies Bergere.** None of the essentials of theatrical showmanship is neglected."

I think that very well proves my point. Although the Fischer show used girls as the theme, with novelty performers working at terrific speed spicing it up, when I utilized the same formula, without the girl feature at all, and used instead a magic theme, even then the Folies Bergere formula was suggested to the reviewer's subconscious mind. Aside from the formula framework, there wasn't a single person or number that even faintly resembled anything in the Fischer show. I got quite a wallop when I read that.

We've already mentioned how a whole act can be built up around a single number, as in the cocktail trick. Ade Duval built up his silk production act from the phantom tube and its variations, originally. You, too, can use a trick as a source of ideas for an act. There are thousands of tricks available for experiment in this direction.

Just by way of illustration, we built up the old water fountain number into an act as a finale for our first part in the International Magicians show:

The curtain opens on an exterior scene with a large tree center stage and beneath it a park bench. The orchestra is playing "Isn't It a Lovely Day to Be Caught In the Rain," and the girl, wearing a bright red cellophane cape, enters with her boy friend who wears a white rain coat. The girl sings the number and at the end, while the orchestra continues softly, she goes to sit on the bench with the boy. There are flashes of lightning and rumbles of thunder.

The boy tries to put his arm around her but she moves away. About this time, unseen by the lovers, a solitary man enters, also clad for rain, and watches the by-play with much interest. The boy tries again, and the girl moves away again. Finally the boy reaches around behind the tree and brings forth a stream of water which fountains into the air from his finger-tips.

He holds the stream of water behind the girl. She, thinking

it is beginning to rain, puts up her umbrella and invites the boy beneath it with her. He grins triumphantly, places the stream on the point of the umbrella and gets beneath it, putting his arm around her.

The bystander snaps his fingers, struck with an idea, and steals the stream from the top of the umbrella, holding it behind his back. Another girl, also dressed in cellophane raincape, enters and starts walking across the stage. But the bystander intercepts her and tips his hat. She tilts up her nose and tries to pass, but the bystander brings the stream of water into play and the girl, too, thinks it is raining and puts up her umbrella, inviting the bystander beneath it with her.

From the opposite side of the stage another girl enters hurriedly, being chased by a masher. The bystander, seeing his predicament, puts the stream of water on the masher's cigarette and pantomimes how to solve his difficulty. He too gets the idea and is presently invited under the third girl's umbrella.

Then a poor old drunk enters, umbrella open, holding out his hand in a vain serch for rain. When the bystander goes over to him the drunk pantomimes his disappointment that it isn't raining. As the drunk holds the umbrella open out in front of him, the bystander deposits the stream on the umbrella's outer perimeter. Delightedly the drunk whirls the umbrella with the stream dancing along its edge.

From another side of the stage comes a girl with a small dog on a leash. The drunk deposits the stream on the dog's back, and the dog goes trotting across the stage to the tree. As he sniffs at the tree trunk, a stream of water squirts from the tree at the dog.

Meanwhile, the orchestra has kept up a musical background of "Isn't It a Lovely Day."

The first girl and her boy friend step forward and the music modulates to "Singing In the Rain." All of the company onstage join in the number and at the climax, with all fountains going, colored lights playing on the streams of water, the curtains close swiftly.

There are so many sources for act ideas that there is really no excuse for lack of one—or a number.

The mere essential of trying to betray human qualities and weaknesses suggests many idea germs.

An act could be planned from the viewpoint of how a drunk sees things. Another could be a demonstration of the psychology of a crazy man. Another act could be based on a serious, but totally meaningless explanation of the Einstein theory. Another could be a mock-serious lecture on what nonsense really is. Still another could be based on the character of a weight guesser, such as is frequently seen at carnivals, fairs and parks. I believe it was Page Wright who published a routine in the Sphinx based on a pitchman. Still another idea could come from the performer teaching the audience how to do card tricks, really teaching them nothing, but still performing tricks which he seems to assume they know how to do. Yet another idea could be based on the performer playing the character of a lawyer explaining how the law works, and using his tricks as the illustrations.

Full evening shows, because of their length of time, should present a variety of ideas in order to retain highest spectator interest.

Don't ever say you can't get an idea for an act. Why there are more ideas for acts than there are—well, magicians, even. And that's a lot.

CHAPTER TWENTY-ONE

There are many mechanical provisions necessary before your act can become a performable reality.

Once the idea has been developed satisfactorily you proceed about the business of getting the materials necessary for the various numbers. **Don't use stock apparatus unless the nature of the act requires it.** Insist that the apparatus look like something in keeping with the idea for the act. As an example: Suppose your idea were built around the egg bag at one stage in the routine. You can buy standard egg bags in black and red and plaid and a great number of colors. Yet they all look like egg bags. They don't look like anything except something a magician would use.

If you are a girl, putting a couple of handles on it and changing its shape to conform to a replica of a woman's hand-bag would bring it into plausible form for use, providing the basic idea of the act would find it consistent for you to have a hand-bag. This was done by Thayer in the bag that accompanies the mutilated parasol trick. He changed the form of the changing bag to appear as a hand-bag.

And for the lord's sake, if you are a he man—I don't mean one of the other kind because the hand-bag might then be in keeping—but if you are a he man, DON'T USE A LADIES' HAND-BAG. And don't use a ladies' parasol for ANY trick, no matter how good the trick. It is out of character—or perhaps it isn't, only you would know. But at least you want to give the impression you are masculine, regardless of your private life.

But to get back to a method of camouflaging the egg bag: Make it look like something a man would have under the circumstances required in the act. I'm afraid I've gotten myself into a corner in the selection of the egg bag for this illustration. It is a random selection, made as I write. Come to think of it there are few bags a man would be found with, and I'm not referring to wives. A tobacco pouch, perhaps. But that might be a bit too small for our purpose. A laundry bag, yes, if a reason can be found to ring in a laundry bag. A paper bag? That might present some difficulties. Perhaps a slipper or shoe bag. But if you can't find a type of bag consistent with the act idea, DIS-CARD THE TRICK AND USE SOMETHING ELSE. After all you merely wish to vanish or produce an egg or something of similar size. There are many ways to do that. And the tricks themselves are positively **only tools.**

Let us assume that you have the properties necessary for your tricks, all consistent with the central idea of the act. Now you prepare the talking material, if the act is to have talk. Have it written, or write it yourself, if you are competent. But be certain it, too, is consistent with the act idea. Now MEMOR-IZE IT.

As you become more and more familiar with the lines, you will find that they flow without effort. Now is the time to begin delivering these lines, not as a recitation, but as **talk,** naturally and in a manner in keeping with the idea of the act. Don't recite. TALK. Talk with ease and fluency, as if the lines were spon-taneous thoughts. This gives freshness.

For the music, it is better if the numbers selected are familiar generally to the public you are to reach, particularly the lyrics, if you wish the music to carry an idea to them. Pro-fessional arrangers, as has been mentioned before, will fit the necessary portions of the music to the length of time necessary to fit the trick it is to accompany. They will also provide for modulations into other numbers.

There is another way this music may be fixed up. You can go to the bigger music stores and purchase orchestrations of the numbers required. Then fit this music to the length of time required. Cut out these portions of the various numbers and paste them up on sheets.

Be sure that the music is carefully cued. On ALL parts mark playing instructions carefully and clearly. Put on definite cues as to when to begin and when to stop, such as "FF until on," "Loudly until on, then very soft until end of handkerchief trick." Then, if you should want to cue a change: "When performer picks up glass box. . ." This means to start the next portion of the music when the performer performs the act indicated.

If there is to be a period of time when the music is to stop you mark the music in this manner: "Cut when performer shows rope restored. Tacit through trick with egg." Tacit means silence. Then, to bring music into the act again: "When performer picks up bottle and glass. . ." If you want the rhythm to fit the action, such as the dancing handkerchief or the bouncing egg, mark: "Catch tempo of bouncing egg (or of dancing handkerchief, whatever applies.)"

If you have percussion cues, mark them both on lead sheet (the sheet used by the director) and on the drum sheet. Typical markings are: "As performer starts bringing large red silk streamer from tube, drum roll crescendo. As end appears, cymbal crash." Or, "Rim shot as each card is dropped."

Remember, neither the leader nor any of his musicians know anything about your act. Give them full instructions. With full instructions, they can play your act as you desire it. The music cues must be explicit and complete.

Assemble all music, marked for proper order, in folders. All of the piano score should go in one folder. All of the violin parts should go in another. And so on. Label the folders on the outside with the name of your act and the instrument for which the parts are.

Leave the music with the musicians until the end of your engagement. But immediately after your last performance go to the leader and get it back. Count all folders and check to see that all music for each instrument has been returned. These pieces get mixed up sometimes with other music.

A cue sheet should also be prepared for the stage manager. This gives all curtain cues, when to open and when to close the curtains. Be specific as to exactly when curtains are to start to close.

A stage electrician's sheet will show all light cues that have to do with the stage switchboard. This means all lighting, including house lights, except for flood and spotlight from the booth. Such light cues resemble the cues on the music. For example: "Open, full up. At performer showing packet of razor blades, stage black." This means all white lights are on until the magician shows a packet of razor blades. When he does this, the stage lights are to be blacked out and the spotlight from the booth will be the only illumination. All instructions for colored illumination are also on this sheet. For example: "1st border blue.

164

2nd border blue and red." This brings blue light in the first row of overhead lights and blue and red in the second row.

If you want the lights to gradually diminish or increase in intensity say: "All whites, (or whatever color desired) on dimmer. Fade whites gradually to end of floating ball trick," or "Gradually bring up white as silks are produced from hat."

If you go into the audience: "House lights up when performer leaves stage—kill, when he returns."

In case of doubt in lighting, err on the side of too much light. The spectators insist on seeing what is going on in a magic act. I remember very well a performance during the act of one of the principals in the International Magicians show. Somehow the light cues got mixed up and the performer was working in a very dimly lit stage. From far out in the darkness of the audience came a complaining bass voice, "He must be on the W. P. A. I can't see him doin' nothin'."

Another cue sheet should be prepared for the spotlight operator in the booth. These instructions must be also complete. Such as, "White spot—Pick up performer at stage R as he enters. Follow. Kill spot on shadow trick. Blue flood during water number."

There should also be a property sheet for the property man. This tells exactly what you want—every table and what is on every table, every chair and every other property you use. AND EXACTLY WHERE IT IS TO BE PLACED. Usually a magician or his assistant sets up his apparatus on his tables exactly where he wants it, and the property man carries it on and places it. These days of fast sequences the magician cannot delay the show and kill time while he monkeys around fiddling with his properties.

So let us assume now that the properties you need are all at hand, the music score is ready, all cue sheets—music, curtains, lights, property sheets—are ready, you have your costume; your lines are committed. There is still one other point. Having decided where each property for each trick is to go, make a map of each table or chair. Show **exactly** where everything is to go. Then make a map of the precise placing of each table or chair. This is for your own guidance as a quick check.

165

Before you go on, make certain that everything is in the proper place. Make certain that the musicians understand how the music is played. Make sure the crew understands how the lights are to be operated. Be certain the stage manner knows the cue for opening and closing the curtain.

Well, here we are. The stage is ready. The music is playing and the curtains are starting open. Go after 'em. Don't forget that you aren't going to sell them tricks. Remember YOU are the important thing here. Get that across to them. Get it across in such a way that when you finish there will be a terrific storm of applause. For YOU. Make 'em want you back. When the applause begins to diminish even the slightest bit—don't wait too long—go out for a bow. Take as many bows as you can.

But don't make the mistake of doing another trick for them. You've got 'em where you want 'em now. Don't risk loosing that smash finish. When they're yelling, clapping, whistling and stamping, you're on top. If you go back and do another trick and they're content to let you finish, you've lost a lot of ground. Quit at the peak.

CHAPTER TWENTY-TWO

There is a certain formula which establishes the shortest route to a career as a successful entertainer, just as there are formulas which point more direct ways to become successful in any other line of endeavor. To say this may seem presumptuous on my part. But successful entertainers have used it. And it has shortened the route to success in other lines.

You have a product to sell. This product is yourself as an entertainer. It is necessary for you to develop an entertainment product that is in great demand. You can learn much, as has been pointed out so often in this work, by studying the leading entertainers in the field you desire to enter. Again I must say, these leading entertainers are NOT magicians—regardless of the field. Today, NO MAGICIAN leads any field—whether it be the lecture field, night-clubs, vaudeville, stage productions, casual dates as at smokers, clubs or banquets. The leading entertainers are invariably some other type.

Automobile manufacturers design their products by watching popular trends. It is no coincidence that practically all cars on the market today are in general quite similar. In investigating them you will find they differ only in minor details. Those cars which are radical departures from the general preferences of the buying public do not sell well. You can check this yourself by comparing the sales volumes of the "freak" cars with competing "conventional" products in the same class.

This also holds true of entertainers.

The successful product is consciously designed to meet the standards set up by the buying public. This absolutely holds true of entertainment as well as automobiles or furniture. Obviously, if you make it the way they want it, they'll buy it.

It was no accident that so many magicians were doing manipulative routines with cards and cigarettes not so long ago. That is the kind of presentation of **magic** the public had seen that they liked and wanted most. Yet they liked and wanted other kinds of entertainment MORE. The box-office and the salaries paid to entertainers proves this. Probably, if magic presentation resembled more the kind of entertainment they liked BEST, some other type of magic, more nearly resembling their preference in general entertainment, would have been more in demand.

This book is almost entirely devoted to an exhaustive study and discussion of general public entertainment preferences. But far more important that this book can be in instructing you on these points would be a personal study on your part of the actual acts themselves. But again and again I must insist, DON'T STUDY MAGIC ACTS. Study the biggest acts or shows, aside from your interest in magic.

See these acts often enough to be able to break them down into their elements. (1) Type of act; (2) Length of act; (3) Type of material used; (4) Type of appeal; (5) Angle of presentation; (6) Dress; (7) Performer's angle or character as shown to audience; (8) Tempo of presentation; (9) Style of presentation; (10) Incidental support like music score; (11) Silent or talking; (12) Just what intrigued the audience; (13) How it was built up.

You might take recently successful magical acts and see how they approach the more generally successful formula. You might try to find out what these acts have in common with the more successful stars. And what they lack.

Regardless of the type of show to which you aspire, you can discover the formula. This holds true of every field whether it be school show, lyceum, full evening show, mental work, private home exhibitions and so on. All you have to do is to discover the essential ingredients in the MOST SUCCESSFUL ENTERTAINERS in that particular field and you can find the formula.

The next step is to sell your booker or agent on you. You have to play up to these fellows. If you can get under their hides——and I mean hides—and become their friends, they will do more for you than if your contacts are purely impersonal. This is only common sense. In the commercial field it is fundamental. Why should it be any different in selling entertainment?

In the commercial field marketing a product is considerably less difficult if it is designed to please the buyers, in this case—until you are booked—the bookers or agents. No matter how good you are, if the bookers don't like you personally, or if they don't like your act, you can't get booked. If you don't get booked, you don't eat. If you dont eat. . .

Now all of this may seem sordidly commercial. It may strike you as the surest way of discouraging individuality and all of that sort of thing. But I said this is the **shortest** route to a successful professional career. It is not the only one.

Perhaps you have the spark of genius. Don't count on this too strongly, however. There are so few geniuses that the odds are decidedly against even you being one. Perhaps you have the insides to battle ahead in the face of rebuff and discouragement. In the long run you will probably make the grade—that is, if you are really exceptional. There always has to be a first to establish a new style or a new slant.

But the latter is the long, hard way.

CHAPTER TWENTY-THREE

Because my International Magicians In Action show expressed my own idea of this modern slant to magical presentation, as best I could under the circumstances at the time, I am including a description of the complete show in its final form, titled in this version, "Magic In the Air." Please do not think that this is the final development in the renaissance in magical presentation which I am certain must ultimately come, if magic is to survive as entertainment. It is merely the first step, in my opinion.

Like all pioneers, we had to use trial-and-error methods, we had to experiment and alter and change. Practically everything which identified the show, as a show, we had to devise ourselves.

Several references to this show have appeared in the various magic magazines, and some few stated that it was modelled upon the usual magical convention show. This, of course, could not be further from the truth. The usual show at a magicians' convention is merely a vaudeville show of magic acts, without regard to any integration. Many times these acts at conventions show marked similarity to other acts. Often convention acts aren't of high calibre as to showmanship and audience appeal.

On the other hand, the principals and their acts were most carefully selected as to the KIND of act and the KIND of people I wanted. Personality came first. Then again, I wanted versatility because I planned on using these principals in ensemble numbers, all working together. This feature alone made it different from convention shows.

In addition all of the acts in some regard varied from the strictly conventional in their own presentation.

At a magicians' convention the illusions are invariably done with the conventional illusions in the conventional manner. There wasn't a conventional illusion in our show, except for one which was kept conventional purposely because its presentation was strictly the reverse.

The general attitude of the magic at a magicians' convention is fooling the customers first, magic for the mystery's sake. We tried to kid the life out of the mystery angle. As a matter of

170

fact the attitude of the whole show was one of kidding magic and magicians and repeatedly the reviewers mentioned the fact that we took neither the audience nor ourselves seriously. That is as it should be. But it is not the case in a convention show.

But more than that there was a sense of unity and integration which carried the show along at terrific speed, with strong contrasts and variety. It was truly a modern revue. The difference between it and most revues was that the usual revue has girls as the theme. Our theme was magic.

We soon discovered that the label "magic show" hurt us badly. Theatre managers were extremely reluctant to book us because of poor experience with conventional magic shows in the past. And when we could get booked it was always at the most disadvantageous terms, which ultimately resulted in wrecking the undertaking.

So we cast about, when the show was revised the last time, for a title which would take that "magic show" curse away from us. Eventually we hit upon the title, "Magic In the Air," which I am now convinced was even worse, because the public confused us with a tab motion picture theatre unit.

I am well aware that these statements as to the bad repute that magic shows have generally, will meet with considerable sharp criticism. But it is true. That was our biggest obstacle. Difficult as the truth may be to bear, when it is extremely unpleasant, nevertheless it should be heard, or steps cannot be taken by magic practitioners generally to overcome the situation.

A few minutes' frank and honest discussion with any professional theatre manager, agent or producer—particularly from the legitimate theatre field—will quite quickly convince you that this situation is only too true. Don't listen to the protests and claims of those who are not in a position to know about this. Don't let examples of extravagant successes impress you either. Many of these successes are not extravagant. Many of them are not successes at all. None of them—and I include everything playing the legitimate field—can compare in any way with competing successes in the theatre field generally.

But to get back to the show itself:

A short, topical lively overture segued immediately into the theme motiv as the curtains were lighted up. Through the split in the front curtain the soprano stepped and sang an eight line prologue. The curtains opened up behind her as she exited.

The scene was a moderne cocktail lounge in a magicians' club and the principals, announced by the soprano, came in singly and in pairs, and had magically produced cigarettes or drinks from the comic bartender. At length the entire company went into the audience doing the miser's dream to the accompaniment of "Pennies From Heaven." At the end the company were all on stage sweeping handfuls of coins from the pails and letting them tumble down. Eventually, we intended to add a shower of bills from the flies and from the center of the audience but this was never included.

The curtains closed upon the principals and immediately reopened on a 4½ minute routine of fast magic done with the performer smartly attired in tails and with his girl assistant in a short costume in black sequins, modelled after a dress suit. The magic was principally cane to silk, gloves to doves and productions of silks and livestock. The act was silent, accompanied by a smart modern musical arrangement.

As the curtains closed a tap-dancing manipulator followed right on, doing a routine with cigarettes, cards and the like. At the end he was dancing on an electrically charged mat which threw flashes of flaming blue fire about the stage.

Without delay of any kind the curtains opened on the memory act with the girl repeating objects written on the blackboard, as called by the audience.

After a short quick comedy bit in one, another principal, also in tails, entered and went into the comedy presentation of the guillotine which ended in a cold pass-out of the comic.

Following this one of the men performed the dancing handkerchief in two, featuring the use of a large glass bottle from which the handkerchief eventually pushed the cork and escaped.

Then in a moderne Oriental setting came a six-minute interval of Chinese magic.

The comics took the stage then and did a ten-minute routine of burlesque magic ending with the Disembodied Princess illusion with the performer's assistant left helplessly without any middle.

"Isn't It a Lovely Day?" was the music theme as the curtains opened upon a garden number, with a girl and boy attired for rain. The girl sang the number and went to sit on the park bench with the boy. Using a fountain of water the boy induces the girl to allow him to get under the umbrella with her, after which several couples become involved with the water until finally the stream is parked on the back of a dog, which when it sniffs a tree trunk, is squirted by the tree. The music changes to "Singing In the Rain," ending with the whole company singing while the fountains are playing in kaliedescopically changing colored lights.

Part Two opened in a Modiste Shop scene with the girls getting the store ready for the day, during which one of the girls made two luminous rag pictures. Discovering a model head upon which is displayed a bridal veil, the girls conclude the original model for the head would have made a lovely bride, whereupon they dress the head which comes to life and walks off stage to the "Wedding March." A girl comes in to buy a bathing suit and the pansy floor-walker arranges for her to try it on behind some hat boxes which he has the girls pile up, all fitting rooms being occupied. But when the floor-walker returns with the bathing suit and realizes that the girl behind the stack of boxes is nude, he knocks over the boxes. But the girl has vanished.

As the curtains close, one of the girls is seen walking across the stage with a tray upon which is a glass of water and a pack of razor blades. One of the performers steps on, stops her and asks her if that isn't his lunch. Then he performs the razor blade silently to musical accompaniment, doing it a white spot.

Following this, a beautiful blond girl magicienne presented a silent routine featuring a strongly built up presentation of a canary trick.

The curtains parted to reveal a party in progress at a cafe. This set was extremely moderne. One of the hostesses passes out squares of tissue and asks all to start tearing when she gives the word. They tear and crush the tissues after which, one by one, the torn papers are seen to have become hats. Each hat is in keeping with the costume of the individual, until it reaches the comic at the end of the line. His papers are revealed to have become a pair of paper panties.

Here the music changes suddenly and a drunk struggles through to the center of the stage. As the others back out of the scene, the drunk goes into his routine. He balances his cane on floor, then smells the lily he is holding. It wilts slowly. He tries to take a cigarette from a packet, but the cigarette rises. His lighter changes to a box of matches. Then he begins seeing drinks. First one, then another and another glass of whiskey appears between his fingers, all to eventually disappear. He hears an alarm clock ring and proceeds to take several from his hat, after which he prepares to go home. His scarf changes color and as he is about to exit he finds a glass of beer in his hands, then two.

There was a short comedy interval in front of the curtains, after which one of the principals came forward and started the murder mystery. He explains that the audience has been appointed to the jury and that a reinactment of the crime will take place. All of the characters are introduced and put on their costumes. But before the scene has gone very far, all of the characters, including the judge, have changed identity and the case is impossible. At the conclusion the cop rushes from the telephone booth wanting to know, "What the hell's going on here?"

After the blackout a vibraharp is seen at one side of the stage and one of the principals enters to play "Stardust." As he goes into the chorus, the curtains behind him slowly part, revealing a lovely girl doing the floating ball. The curtains close behind the musician on the last note of music.

One of the girls steps out in one and begins singing "Castle of Dreams," and at the end of the first chorus the curtains part behind her showing her boy friend with a model of their love-nest. After showing it to her, the girl asks the boy if there has ever been another woman in his life. When he says no, the roof of the miniature house is lifted and another gal stands up saying, "The same old line, eh, daddy?" Blackout.

A Mexican steps out in front of the olio and does the cut rope, almost getting into trouble before it is successfully concluded. Then he lies down for a nap. The curtains part, revealing a hacienda and the Mexican's tired wife sitting dejectedly on a large trunk which she has carried many miles. Several tourists enter and it soon becomes evident that the Mexican is a very lazy person. But when comment is made along that line, he volunteers to show them the fastest trick in the world. Comfortably at his ease, the Mexican directs that steel plates be put on all sides within the trunk, but while this is being done, three very disreputable-looking natives stick their heads over the top of the adobe wall and are promptly shot down by the Mexican. He explains that they are his brothers and that they are always trying to steal his tricks. He spots a good-looking girl with the tourists and decides to do the trick with her, sending his wife home. The trunk is securely roped and locked, with the "gringo" girl safely tied inside a sack with it. Suddenly the Mexican dives within the canopy which has been erected over the trunk, and almost instantaneously the canopy is removed disclosing the gringo girl running about in bewilderment. The Mexican is found within the sack, inside the trunk smoking a cigarette.

Immediately following, one of the principals enters and says that the audience is now going to be given an opportunity to determine who is the greatest magician in the world. He no sooner has the words out of his mouth than the performers, one after another, enter each with a bigger megaphone than the one ahead, insisting that they are the greatest magicians in the world.

The curtains swing open and a stageful of apparatus is disclosed. All of the performers leap for the apparatus. There is a bewildering three minutes of productions of all kinds—clocks, bowls of water, ducks, chickens, pigeons, silks, flowers, after which a loud shot is heard off stage. A girl comes in dressed as a rabbit, insisting that she is the rabbit and doesn't care who is the greatest magician in the world. Whereupon the rabbit takes a miniature magician out of the hat.

CHAPTER TWENTY-FOUR

Now that we are approaching the end of our discussion, it might be well to stop and take inventory of what has been developed herein without the accompanying reasons and explanation.

It has been made quite clear, I hope, that ultimate success as an entertainer, whether you wish to spend all of your time at it as a professional or whether your appearances are limited to strictly occasional shows, rests upon your ability to **sell yourself.** That selling yourself is more important than selling your magic. This holds true whether you perform for a lone friend at home, or in a theatre seating hundreds.

Stress the qualities and behavior that will accentuate likeable and audience-attracting characteristics. Emphasize humor, courtesy, liking for people, friendliness, happiness and good disposition. Be generous, accommodating, affable and patient. Show consideration for your assistants, both volunteer and professional. Try to get as many sympathetic ties with your audience as possible.

Don't try to sell them on how clever or smart you are. Don't be competitive or combative or vain. Don't boast or brag. Don't swear or lose your temper. During your performance don't be weak and ineffectual. Don't look for things. Don't fumble and mumble and forget. Don't allow any awkward pauses.

Know what you are to do, how to do it. And do it with the least delay, every time you do a trick.

Your grooming should be faultless. Your properties should be clean and well cared for. Treat your assistants as individual humans, not as automatons. Emphasize comedy and music and rhythm. Make your attack lively. Give your act lift—always.

See that your personal demeanor is excellent. Be at ease, confident and friendly. Stay away from arrogance and conceit.

Prepare your act thoroughly and well, and provide for smooth operation in all departments including music, lighting and staging, if it is a stage appearance.

Don't be familiar or fresh.

Be sure your act is well lighted and that the audience can see everything you do. Make certain they can understand every word and every expression.

Review the extensive lists of audience appeals again and again, even though your act may be complete. Every time you can add one of those magnetic sales points, add it—even if it takes some trouble.

Don't talk too fast. Don't talk too loud. Don't talk in a high-pitched, strained voice.

Don't use small props. Don't do anything that all can't see clearly. View your own props at a distance. Make certain they can be seen well. Often poor color combinations lower the visibility, through lack of contrast to accentuate other parts of the apparatus. Or because the props are obscured because they blend with the background.

Don't do too many card tricks where identification of particular cards is the feature. This confines the routine to too few people.

Don't scowl. SMILE. Smile all of the time.

Don't turn your back to the audience.

Don't allow any waits, either before starting your act or during your routine.

When you bow, bow from the hips—not the neck. Bow forward, easily and gracefully, with your hands hanging easily at your sides. When you bow, don't bend your legs.

When you finish a number, make it clear to the audience you have finished. Await their applause. It will come.

As you reach a climax, gradually ritard your talking and action, ritarding your music as well—slower and slower. At the end, bring up both the music and the lights in a crescendo.

When you begin, start briskly and with eagerness. Try every device you can to "hook" the audience's attention, interest and liking. Try to do it from the very start.

During your routine, look at your audience and smile occasionally. Don't look at one place all of the time. Give your attention to many parts of the audience.

Show everything you are to use clearly and plainly. If there is any doubt as to whether the spectators know what you are to use, TELL THEM IN THAT MANY WORDS.

Where you are working to a wide audience, shift your position occasionally so that all may participate.

Before you include any operation that will take up time unnecessarily, be certain that the lull will be more than made up for in what follows. Things that take up time and are best left out of modern routines are such thing as: (1) Having spectators come up to the stage; (2) Borrowing things from the audience; (3) Giving out pieces of apparatus or properties for examination—practically all of this is unnecessary; (4) Having cards selected or other objects identified.

NEVER END YOUR ACT OR SHOW WITH A SPECTATOR ON THE STAGE. The necessary wait for his return to his seat will ruin your climax and the applause.

Here is a whole work on showmanship, yet so far it hasn't been defined. Really, it takes all of the words that have gone before to define it. That's what this book is—just a definition of showmanship.

From all of the foregoing it must be evident by now that showmanship is accenting and accentuating the important parts of your act, bringing out the points clearly and deliberately, just as you accent important words in your everyday speech. Showmanship is the portraying of likeable characters, and likeable human qualities. It is in emphasizing the difficulty of something so that it seems more difficult, thus emphasizing your skill. It is emphasizing the danger in the situation, so as to enhance your daring. It is to emphasize every quality—comedy, music and all of the others—so that the audience will like you more.

Really, showmanship is merely skillful emphasis. It is skillful emphasis combined with good solid bedrock psychology.

One final reminder: As you would avoid "dated" or outmoded clothing, keep your presentation and all connected with it in the manner of the present fashion.

It is unnecessary to remind you, I hope, that you should never leave the sight of the audience during your performance, never leave the stage except for quick trips into the audience where you may be plainly seen and clearly heard.

And finally: THESE GENERAL RULES OF SHOWMANSHIP SHOULD BE APPLIED—INSOFAR AS POSSIBLE—TO ALL OF YOUR PERFORMING APPEARANCES, WHETHER

FOR A SMALL GROUP AT HOME, AT A CLUB, IN A NIGHT SPOT OR AT A THEATRE.

THESE RULES ARE FOR MAKING MAGIC ENTERTAINING TO YOUR SPECTATORS UNDER ALL CIRCUMSTANCES.

Before we leave you, let's consider that act you are using now. Has it really been clicking? Does it get the audience response you desire? Or do other acts on the bill register far more strongly than you do?

Everything that has gone before in this book is directed at making your act—the very act you are now doing—more pleasing to your audiences. Incorporate those audience preferences in your present routine without further delay. Don't wait until you can add ALL of them. It isn't possible to include all of them in any act.

Include as many as you can—one at a time, if necessary. But start right in today broadening the appeal of your routine.

These features, explained to you in such detail, are not mere theories. They are FACTS. They are the real secrets of the show business. They are much more important secrets than the secrets you, as a magician, so preciously guard when you seek to prevent exposure of magicians' methods.

I can prove it to you, if you will let me.

Of course, it is necessary that I assume you can successfully present the tricks you use. I mean that you know how to operate them so that the effect desired is accomplished. I must assume, too, that you are technically capable of executing the various sleights. I must assume, too, that you can perform the tricks well, without uncertainty or blundering. If you can't, there are portions of this work that tell you how to overcome those difficulties.

So . . . Now you have a smooth, carefully and thoroughly rehearsed routine. You can do it well.

Tonight. Cut one of those tricks out. Eliminate the weakest one, or the one that seems not to fit into the routine well.

If you have the time, and can do it without complicating matters too much, deliberately add one or more of the audience appeals. But at any rate toss out at least one trick. Make the the act one trick shorter than you think it should be.

Do it that way tonight.

I think you will agree tomorrow that the audience liked you better. I say this with much confidence because the average magician is on too long and does too much. All of them don't kill themselves off with their audiences, but fully ninety percent do. That's why I think that one expedient will help you.

And tomorow night, try eliminating another. Keep this up until you find the audience hasn't had enough of you. This FORCES applause because if they haven't had enough, **they'll applaud for more.**

It's just a suggestion that you might find helpful.

And now on getting applause:

The first rule, of course, is to make them want more because you haven't given them enough. The next rule is to let them know you are finished. BE SURE TO INDICATE UNMISTAKABLY THAT YOU ARE APPROACHING THE END OF YOUR TRICK OR THE END OF YOUR ACT. After you have shown them you are approaching the end, SHOW THEM YOU ARE NOW AT THE END. Then, SHOW THEM YOU HAVE FINISHED.

It is done in three steps: (1) Showing the approach of the end; (2) Indicating the end; (3) Clearly point out that you have finished.

Then deliberately wait for the applause. Wait ten seconds or more, if necessary. But wait. The applause will come. Look right at the audience. AND JUST WAIT. Even if you aren't good, someone will start to applaud and others will follow.

Will you try this also? Tonight?

CHAPTER TWENTY-FIVE

As a means of checking various stages of your act and to make it possible to compare notes quickly, I have included the following check lists for your convenience.

Check Chart—Audience Appeals

1—Music
2—Rhythm
3—Movement
4—Sex Appeal
5—Youth
6—Personality
7—Color
8—Comedy
9—Harmony
10—Romance
11—Sentiment
12—Nostalgia
13—Pointing
14—Timing
15—Surprise
16—Situation
17—Character
18—Conflict
19—Proper costuming
20—Careful grooming
21—Physical action
22—Group coordination
23—Precise attack
24—Short turns or scenes
25—Efficient pacing
26—Punch
27—Careful routining
28—Tireless rehearsal
29—Special material
30—Grace

31—Effortless skill
32—Surefire material
33—Spectacle
34—Thrill
35—Emotion
36—Common problems
37—Escape from the humdrum
38—Unity
39—Up-to-dateness

Check Chart—Act Idea

1—What is basic theme of act?

2—What character do you play? To crystallize your own concept, define character as to

        a—Age
        b—Education
        c—Locale of birth
        d—Ambitions
        e—Virtues
        f—Faults and weaknesses
        g—Beliefs, etc.

3—Costume

        a—Coat
        b—Trousers
        c—Shirt
        d—Shoes
        e—Accessories

4—What is character's purpose in action of act?
5—What tricks are to be used?
6—How are they tied to the act idea?
7—What is the principal audience appeal?
8—List all other appeals.
9—List music to accompany each trick.
10—Write down general theme or spoken part.
11—List all punches.
12—Which is the big punch for act's end?
13—How many audience appeals are at the climax?

14—Can you add more?

15—Can you add more audience appeals anywhere in the act?

16—What is your opening?

17—How will it "hook" audience interest?

18—For what type of audience is act intended?

19—What is that audience's chief interest?

20—What interest and attention appeals are incorporated in the act?

21—Can you add more?

22—Is your general idea of the act similar in framework to some outstanding act?

23—What is the general outline of the pattern act?

24—What is the general parallel outline of your act?

25—How long will your act run?

26—How long will each number run?

27—Can you cut the time?

    a—By shortening the numbers

    b—By elminating unnecessary waits

    c—By eliminating explanations or briefing them

    d—By eliminating non-essential numbers

28—Are the technical requirements within your capacity?

29—Eliminate ALL MATERIAL intended only for killing time.

Check Chart—Routine

1—List all numbers in their proper order.

2—List all properties in their proper order.

3—List all music in its proper order.

4—List all lights in their proper order.

5—Make map of placing of tables and large props.

6—Make map of all properties on tables and chairs.

7—Prepare or have prepared all talking material.

8—Coordinate all talking material to program.

9—Coordinate to program all properties and necessary handling.

10—Make map of final placement of properties AFTER use.

11—Time all numbers.

12—Eliminate everything that does not advance act.

13—Provide music score coordinated to program.

14—Arrange for costumes.

15—Arrange for assistants' costumes.

16—Arrange for assistants.

17—Cue sheet for assistants.

18—How can assistants be emphasized as people?

19—Where will assistants be at each moment of each number?

20—How will you enter?

21—Where will you enter?

22—How will you exit?

23—Where will you exit?

24—Where will assistants be at close of act or show?

25—How long does act run?

26—Does it exceed the acceptable time for that class of audience?

27—Does act move swiftly?

28—Does it lift?

29—Does each minor point build towards the climax?

30—Check for timing.

31—Check for pointing.

32—Rehearse thoroughly with all props.

33—Rehearse thoroughly with all costumes, music and props.

34—Rehearse thoroughly without further changes.

35—Watch voice placement.

36—Watch tempo of delivery.

37—When act is within proper time, rehearse thoroughly with music, costumes and all props until you can do it subconsciously.

38—Make complete list of all items necessary for performing, and check it before leaving for your engagement.

      a—Music score

      b—Cue sheets

      c—All tricks

      d—All trick accessories, including perishables

      e—Costumes—(Complete details.)

      f—Costume accessories (Complete details.)

      g—Make-up

      h—Towels, kleenex, etc., for cleaning up before and after performance i—Comb and brush

j—Emergency repair kit—scissors, tacks, glue, needle, thread, pliers, small hammer, pins, etc.

k—Shoe brush or cloth

l—Clothes brush

m—Clothing hangers

Check Chart—Performance

1—Check list of required items before leaving for engagement.

2—Give music score to director.

3—Rehearse music with orchestra until all cues are clear.

4—Give stage manager curtain cue sheet.

5—Make sure it is clear to stage manager.

6—Give electrician cue sheets for stage and booth lighting.

7—Make sure light cues are clear.

8—Give prop list and instructions to prop man.

9—Make certain prop requirements are clear.

10—Find place on the bill.

11—Be ready in ample time.

12—Have clothes pressed.

13—Hang up costumes early, to allow wrinkles to come out.

14—Make-up carefully.

15—Clean hands well before going on.

16—Lay out all props ready for performance

17—Mentally go over entire program and check props as you do.

18—Be relaxed, calm, confident.

19—Brush clothing.

20—Wipe off shoes.

Check Chart—After Performance

1—Get music score and check it.

2—Get all cue sheets.

3—Check all properties and pack carefully.

4—Pack costumes carefully.

5—Leave dressing room clean.

6—Be certain to bid good-bye to chairman, manager or other person responsible for your engagement. Express pleasure at having played for him and thank him.

7—Make notes of all unexpected audience responses.

8—Make notes of all numbers that failed to register as expected.

9—Make notes of weakest numbers.

10—Make notes of any mistakes you made.

11—Make notes of any mistakes in the music.

12—Make notes of any mistakes in the lights.

Check Chart—Act Revisions

1—Correct any mistakes in previous performance.

2—Correct cue sheets and music score to eliminate mistakes in previous performances.

3—Try to replace weakest numbers with stronger substitutes.

4—Try to discover why expected responses did not come.

    a—Check timing and pointing.

    b—Check location on program.

    c—Try to add more audience interests.

    d—Make certain you were understood and that all was clearly visible.

    e—Make certain number and interpretation were not inconsistent or out of place.

5—Find out reasons for unexpected response.

    a—Try to increase this.

    b—Is it an important hint for rearrangement?

6—Were any new ideas suggested by performing experience, for strenghtening act or show?

7—Was your entrance effective?

8—Was your act smooth?

9—Was the applause sufficient?

10—Were other acts better received?

    a—If so, why?

    b—Can you see how you can improve your reception?

11—Was your final punch effective?

12—Was your bow well done? Your exit smooth?

13—Can you further strengthen audience appeal?

    a—By your own demeanor

    b—By adding new audience preference factors

    c—By lengthening your act

    d—By shortening your act

e—By tightening your act

f—By further rehearsals

g—By changes of any kind

14—Before your next performance make certain all mistakes are eliminated and all new improvements are incorporated, routined and thoroughly rehearsed.

Check Chart—Applause

1—Did you establish all of your punches clearly?

2—Did you leave the audience wanting more?

3—As you approached the end of each trick did you

a—**Clearly** show the end was approaching?

b—Make it **unmistakable** when the end came?

c—Definitely show you had finished?

4—Did you wait for your applause deliberately, looking at the audience?

5—At the end of your act did you take the three steps necessary to show the conclusion of the act?

a—Show when the end was approaching?

b—Definitely indicate the end?

c—Clearly show you had finished?

6—After your exit, if the applause still continued, did you **promptly** return for a bow?

CPSIA information can be obtained
at www.ICGtesting.com
Printed in the USA
BVHW04s0846090518
515742BV00002B/96/P

9 781684 221066